How to Pray in the Spirit

How to Pray in the Spirit

John Bunyan

WORD PUBLISHING
Word (UK) Ltd
Milton Keynes, England
WORD AUSTRALIA
Kilsyth, Victoria, Australia
WORD COMMUNICATIONS LTD
Vancouver, B.C., Canada
STRUIK CHRISTIAN BOOKS (PTY) LTD
Maitland, South Africa
ALBY COMMERCIAL ENTERPRISES PTE LTD
Balmoral Road, Singapore
CHRISTIAN MARKETING NEW ZEALAND LTD
Havelock North, New Zealand
JENSCO LTD
Hong Kong
SALVATION BOOK CENTRE
Malaysia

HOW TO PRAY IN THE SPIRIT

ISBN 0-85009-513-1 (Australia ISBN 1-86258-162-2)

Reproduced, printed and bound in Great Britain for Word (UK)
Ltd. by Clays Ltd, St Ives plc.

91 92 93 94 / 10 9 8 7 6 5 4 3 2 1

JOHN BUNYAN ON PRAYER

Prayer is a sincere, sensible, affectionate pouring out of your heart or soul to God, through Jesus Christ, in the strength and assistance of the Holy Spirit, for such things as God has promised, or according to the Word of God, for the good of the Church, with submission in faith to the will of God.

From Bedford Prison
1662

CONTENTS

A Month of Devotions on Praying in the Power of the Holy Spirit

HOW TO PRAY IN THE SPIRIT

BY

JOHN BUNYAN

Author of the Christian classics

The Pilgrim's Progress, The Holy War, and *Grace Abounding*

Compiled and Edited for Today's Readers by

L. G. Parkhurst, Jr.

INTRODUCTION

John Bunyan was born near Bedford, England, in 1628. A poor, uneducated tinker, he could barely read when he was converted to Christ, and then called into the Christian ministry. His love for God's Word motivated him to learn to read well, and he began to write prolifically with his Bible in his hands. He worked for religious freedom in England, and in 1660, he was imprisoned for preaching in public. From his lonely prison cell, Bunyan learned how to pray and found the Holy Spirit was truly his Comforter. From that same cell, he was inspired to write not only the words that comprise this book, but also the great Christian classic, *The Pilgrim's Progress.*

In 1662, he wrote his thoughts on prayer: thoughts forged on the anvil of religious persecution. His wife had struggled in vain to win his release from Bedford Prison in 1661, and he faced an indefinite future. He took comfort from two books in his possession during the writing of these meditations on prayer: the Bible and *Fox's Book of Martyrs.* He learned from these books that the only way to glorify God in his sufferings, even if he were destined for the scaffold, was to attend "God's School of Prayer", to pray often and deeply. What he learned about prayer he carefully recorded, and then he passed the sheets of his manuscript through the prison bars to encourage his wife and those facing persecution, prison, and death outside his prison cell. After Bunyan was released from prison in 1672, he returned to public preaching and continued to write. He died in 1688.

I have edited and updated the language of his writings on prayer into these daily meditations for today's English reader. Following each meditation, I have written my own prayer. I hope my prayers will encourage you to pray your own prayers, applying Bunyan's principles to your situation. You will find Bunyan's meditations to be simple, direct, and rich in Scripture and its application. He used repetition wisely to firmly implant his central ideas into the heart and mind of his readers, and I have continued his practice in these devotions.

I have also adopted Bunyan's purpose in editing these meditations. Bunyan wants us to pray in both spirit and mind. He wants to encourage us to pray in a reasonable fashion according to the Scriptures and under the Holy Spirit's power and leading. As Bunyan condemned the mechanicalness, the heartlessness and the hypocrisy that can attend the use of many prayer books or prayer techniques, so I hope that *How to Pray in the Spirit* will grant you greater insight and freedom of expression in your personal relationship with God through Jesus Christ. I hope that you will never need to rely upon someone else's printed prayers as your only access to the throne of grace, but will discover the power and presence of the Holy Spirit who will direct us to pray acceptably to God.

With Love in the Risen Lamb of God,
L. G. Parkhurst, Jr.
1991

HOW TO PRAY IN THE

SPIRIT

BY

JOHN BUNYAN

— 1 —

TRUE PRAYER

God commands us to pray. He commands us to pray in public and in private. Prayer brings those who have the spirit of supplication into a wonderful communion and fellowship with God; therefore, God has ordained prayer as a means for us to grow in a personal relationship with Him.

When we pray often and actively, our prayers acquire great things from God, both for those for whom we pray as well as for ourselves. Prayer opens our heart to God. Our prayers are the means by which our souls, though empty, are filled by God to overflowing. In our prayers, we Christians can open our hearts to God as to a friend, and obtain a fresh confirmation of His friendship with us.

I might spend many words in distinguishing between public and private prayer. I might also distinguish between prayer in the heart and prayer that is spoken aloud. Something also might be said regarding the differences between the gifts and the graces of prayer. But I have chosen to make it my business to show you only the very heart of prayer, without which all your lifting up, both of hands and eyes and voices, will be to no purpose at all.

We must learn and apply what the Scriptures teach. Paul wrote and gave us an example, "I will pray with the Spirit." Therefore, I will tell you: first, what true prayer is; second, what it is to pray with the Holy Spirit; third, what it is to pray with the Spirit and with the mind; and fourth, what are some uses and applications of what I have explained about prayer.

True prayer is a sincere, sensible, affectionate pouring out of your heart or soul to God, through Jesus Christ, in the strength and assistance of the Holy Spirit, for such things as God has promised, or according to the Word of God, for the good of the Church, with submission in faith to the will of God.

This definition includes seven things which I must discuss in detail in the following pages. First, your prayers must be sincere. Second, your prayers must be sensible. Third, your prayers must be an affectionate pouring out of your soul to God the Father through Jesus Christ. Fourth, if you want your prayers to be effective, you must pray by the strength and assistance of the Holy Spirit. Fifth, for your prayers to be answered according to the will of God, you must pray for such things as God has promised, or according to His Word, the Bible. Sixth, your prayers should not be selfish, but should keep in view the good of the Church as well as others. Seventh, you should always pray in faith and with submission to the will of God.

PRAYER

Oh God, the pressures of my busy life weigh upon me, and I confess that I have not taken the time to develop a deep familiarity and fellowship with You. I have not really

16

opened my heart to You, nor have I taken the time to know by experience the openness of Your heart to me. Help me over these next several days to take the time to learn about true prayer from a man who was mastered by the Holy Spirit in prayer, who knew what it was to learn of You behind prison walls. Help me to pray in order to know You better. Help me to pray so I might be empowered to witness before those who need to accept the truth of the Gospel of Your precious Son, for His sake I pray. Amen.

— 2

SINCERE PRAYER

I must remind you that:

Prayer is a *sincere*, sensible, affectionate pouring out of your heart or soul to God, through Jesus Christ, in the strength and assistance of the Holy Spirit, for such things as God has promised, or according to the Word of God, for the good of the Church, with submission in faith to the will of God.

Remember, your prayers must always *sincerely* pour out your heart or soul to God. Sincerity is a grace that runs through all the graces of God in us. Sincerity should control and run through all the actions of a Christian. If your actions are not sincere, then God will not approve your actions.

What must be true regarding sincere actions will be equally true of prayer. David speaks of this when he mentions his own prayers: "I cried out to him," to the Lord, "with my mouth; his praise was on my tongue. If I had cherished sin in my heart, the Lord would not have listened; but God has surely listened and heard my voice in prayer" (Psalm 66:17-19).

Sincerity is a crucial element in prayer. Unless we are sincere, God will not look upon our words as prayer in the good sense:

> I said to the Lord, "You are my Lord;
> apart from you I have no good thing."
> As for the saints who are in the land,
> they are the glorious ones in whom is all my
>   delight.
> The sorrows of those will increase
> who run after other gods.
> I will not pour out their libations of blood
> or take up their names on my lips.
> (Psalm 16:1-4)

And God also tells us, "Then you will call upon me and come and pray to me, and I will listen to you. You will seek me and find me when you seek me with all your heart" (Jeremiah 29:12,13).

The Lord has rejected many prayers for their lack of sincerity. Through the prophets, God said, "They do not cry out to me from their hearts" that is, in sincerity, "but wail upon their beds" (Hosea 7:14). Their prayers were pretentious. Their prayers were hypocritical, a mere show to be seen by others. They prayed to be applauded for their loud prayers.

Jesus Christ commended Nathanael for his sincerity when he was seated under the fig tree. We read: "When Jesus saw Nathanael approaching, he said of him, 'Here is a true Israelite, in whom there is nothing false' " (John 1:47). I suppose this good man was pouring out his soul to God in prayer under the fig tree. Jesus knew he prayed with a sincere and unfeigned spirit before the Lord. Sincerity is one of the principal ingredients in prayer that influences God to hear and consider it. Thus, "The Lord detests the sacrifice of the wicked, but the prayer of the upright pleases him" (Proverbs 15:8).

Why must sincerity be an essential element of acceptable prayer to God? Because sincerity moves you in all simplicity to open your heart to God and to tell Him your case plainly and without equivocation. Sincerity in prayer motivates your heart to condemn your sin plainly, without concealing the facts, intentions or feelings under false excuses and pretences.

When we pray from the heart, we cry to God heartily without complimenting ourselves or praising our righteousness. The Lord declared to Jeremiah the prophet:

> "I have surely heard Ephraim's moaning:
> 'You disciplined me like an unruly calf,
> and I have been disciplined.
> Restore me, and I will return,
> because you are the Lord my God.
> After I strayed,
> I repented;
> after I came to understand,
> I beat my breast.
> I was ashamed and humiliated
> because I bore the disgrace of my youth.' "
> (Jeremiah 31:18,19)

Sincerity is always the same in a person, whether he is praying in a corner all alone or praying before the whole world. Sincerity does not know how to wear two different masks, one for an appearance before others and another for a short span in a corner before God. Sincere Christians must have *God*. They must be with Him in what they know as the pleasant duty of prayer from the heart.

Sincere prayer is not lip-labour, because God looks at the heart. Prayer from the heart looks at God. Prayer from the heart and soul which God regards is that prayer from His children which is accompanied with sincerity.

PRAYER

Oh Lord, my God, may I be found of You as Jesus found Nathanael along the way, in sincere and in utterly devoted prayer to You. I confess that some of my motives for prayer have been selfish and self-seeking. I confess that I have often not taken the time to examine my heart and open it completely before You in prayer. Instead, I have come asking only for the things that I want You to do for me. I bow before You now, O Lord, in humble submission, and I ask You to make in me a clean heart and put a right spirit within me. As I examine my own heart, I come to You in complete sincerity that I would be known of You and You would be known of me, that Your Son might commend me when we meet, that there would be nothing false in me, that I might also feel free to pray in the Saviour's Name knowing that I am cleansed by His atoning blood. Amen.

— 3 —————————

HOW TO PRAY FOR MERCY

Prayer is a sincere, *sensible*, affectionate pouring out of the heart or soul to God, through Christ, in the strength and assistance of the Holy Spirit, for such things as God has promised, or according to the Word of God, for the good of the Church, with submission in faith to the will of God.

Prayer is not a few babbling, prating, complimentary expressions, but a reasonable feeling in the heart. Prayer is sensible of many different things. Sometimes we pray with a sense of sin, sometimes with a sense of mercy needed or received, and sometimes with a sense that God is ready to give us mercy and forgiveness.

Because we understand the danger of sin, in prayer we often sense our need of mercy. Our soul feels. From

23

feeling, our soul will sigh, groan, and break in our heart. Right prayer can bubble up out of the heart when it is pressed with grief and bitterness. When Hannah prayed for a child, the Bible says, "In bitterness of soul Hannah wept much and prayed to the Lord," and the Lord heard her prayer and she conceived and gave birth to the great prophet Samuel (1 Samuel 1:10).

David described some of his prayers by saying, "I am worn out calling for help; my throat is parched. My eyes fail, looking for my God" (Psalm 69:3). David roars, weeps, faints at heart, and fails at the eyes: "I am feeble and utterly crushed; I groan in anguish of heart. All my longings lie open before you, O Lord; my sighing is not hidden from you. My heart pounds, my strength fails me; even the light has gone from my eyes" (Psalm 38:8-10).

Hezekiah mourns like a dove: "I cried like a swift or thrush, I moaned like a mourning dove. My eyes grew weak as I looked at the heavens. I am troubled; O Lord, come to my aid" (Isaiah 38:14). Ephraim moans before the Lord and the Lord hears his cry: "I have surely heard Ephraim's moaning" (Jeremiah 31:18).

In the New Testament, we find the same things. Peter weeps bitterly: "Then Peter remembered the word Jesus had spoken: 'Before the rooster crows, you will disown me three times.' And he went outside and wept bitterly" (Matthew 26:75). Christ had strong cryings and tears in His prayers: "During the days of Jesus' life on earth, he offered up prayers and petitions with loud cries and tears to the one who could save him from death, and he was heard because of his reverent submission" (Hebrews 5:7). Christ cried and wept all from a sense of the justice of God, the guilt of sin, and the pains of hell and destruction.

We find great solace from the Psalms as they express our inner sensibility in prayer:

> I love the Lord, for he heard my voice;
> he heard my cry for mercy.
> Because he turned his ear to me,
> I will call on him as long as I live.
> The cords of death entangled me,
> the anguish of the grave came upon me;

24

I was overcome by trouble and sorrow.
Then I called on the name of the Lord:
"O Lord, save me! " (Psalm 116:1-4).

In all the instances mentioned here, and in hundreds more that might be named from the Scriptures, you may see that prayer carries within it a sensible, feeling disposition, and often it has a sense of the awfulness of sin.

When your prayers are a sincere and sensible pouring out of your heart and soul to God, then sometimes you will receive a sweet sense of mercy received: encouraging, comforting, strengthening, enlivening and enlightening mercy. Thus David pours out his soul to bless and praise and admire the great God for His loving kindness to such poor vile sinners:

> Praise the Lord, O my soul,
> and forget not all his benefits—
> who forgives all your sins
> and heals all your diseases;
> who redeems your life from the pit
> and crowns you with love and compassion,
> who satisfies your desires with good things,
> so that your youth is renewed like the eagle's.
> (Psalm 103:2-5)

The prayers of the saints are sometimes turned into praise and thanksgiving. This is a great mystery: God's people pray with their praises, as it is written:

> Rejoice in the Lord always. I will say it again: Rejoice! Let your gentleness be evident to all. The Lord is near. Do not be anxious about anything, but in everything, by prayer and petition, with thanksgiving, present your requests to God. And the peace of God, which transcends all understanding, will guard your hearts and your minds in Christ Jesus (Philippians 4:4-7).

When you pray to God with a sensible thanksgiving

for the mercies you have received from His hand, your prayer is a mighty prayer in the sight of God. Such a prayer prevails with Him unspeakably.

Sometimes in prayer, our soul has a sense of the mercy we need to receive. This sets our soul aflame as David prayed:

> O Lord Almighty, God of Israel, you have revealed this to your servant, saying, " I will build a house for you." So your servant has found courage to offer you this prayer. O Sovereign Lord, you are God! Your words are trustworthy, and you have promised these good things to your servant. (2 Samuel 7:27,28)

Jacob, David, Daniel and others were given a sense that God wanted to bless them. This prompted them to pray, not by fits and starts, not in a foolish frothy way to babble over a few words written on paper, but mightily, fervently, and continually to groan out their situation before the Lord, as being sensible, *sensible* I say, of their needs, their misery, and the willingness of God to show them His mercy.

PRAYER

O Lord, I sometimes moan under the agony of unrepented and unconfessed sin; forgive me for thinking that I could hide my innermost thoughts from You. I do moan when I see the horrible effects which sin has had upon my life and upon the lives of others. I do moan and agonise over the state of this fallen world and over the evil inflicted upon it by the heartless and cruel enemies of Your Kingdom. I pray for mercy now, and I ask You to assure me by Your Word that the victory is indeed already won through faith in Jesus Christ.

Lord, even as I pray, I praise You and thank You for the precious promises of Scripture that I can apply to the needs and even groanings of my daily life. I praise You that through the sacrifice You made on the cross, I have received mercy upon mercy both in this life and in the life to come.

Use my afflictions, O God, to demonstrate Your love and power and wisdom and faithfulness, even to the praise of Your glory. Amen.

— 4 ——————

PRAYER MUST BE AFFECTIONATE

Prayer is a sincere, sensible, *affectionate* pouring out of the heart or soul to God, through Christ, in the strength and assistance of the Holy Spirit, for such things as God has promised, or according to the Word of God, for the good of the Church, with submission in faith to the will of God.

Oh! the heat, strength, life, vigour and affection that you will find in right prayer! Can you pray these psalms from your heart? "As the deer pants for streams of water, so my soul pants for you, O God" (Psalm 42:1). "How I long for your precepts! Preserve my life in your righteousness" (Psalm 119:40). "I long for your salvation, O Lord, and your law is my delight" (Psalm 119:174). "My soul yearns, even faints, for the courts of the Lord; my heart and my flesh cry out for the living God" (Psalm 84:2). "My soul is consumed with longing for your laws at all times" (Psalm 119:20). Notice this prayer: "My soul is consumed with longing." Oh! what affection there must be in prayer!

You will find a similar devotion with Daniel: "O Lord, listen! O Lord, forgive! O Lord, hear and act! For your sake, O my God, do not delay, because your city and your people bear your Name" (Daniel 9:19). Every syllable carries a mighty vehemence and urgency in it. This is called the fervent, or the working prayer, by the Apostle James. And so again it is reported of Jesus, "And being in anguish, he prayed more earnestly, and his sweat was like drops of blood falling to the ground" (Luke 22:44).

Jesus had His affections more and more drawn out after God for His helping hand. Oh! how far away from the Bible's example are most people when they pray. In God's reckoning, prayer must be with earnestness and urgency. Alas! the greatest number of people have no conscience at all about the duty of prayer; and as for those who do, I fear that many of them are great strangers to the sincere, sensible, and affectionate pouring out of their hearts or souls to God. Too many content themselves with a little lip-service and bodily exercises, mumbling over a few imaginary prayers. When your affections are indeed engaged, and engaged in such urgency that your soul will spend itself to nothing, as it were, rather than go without the good desired, you will have communion and solace with Christ. And hence it is that the saints have spent their strength, and lost their lives, rather than go without the blessing God intended for them.

PRAYER

Dear Father, I love You with my whole heart and being. You have given me life and light in Jesus Christ. You have given me a world where all creation points to You and to Your divine character and grace. You have given me the opportunity to join with all the saints in prayer for the Church and for her establishment in every corner of the earth. I long to see You in all of Your beauty and excellence,

30

and that longing strengthens me in my pilgrimage. I long for Your coming again in power and glory. I long for the redemption of all creation, that is groaning to be released from its bondage to decay. I take delight in the promise that there will be a time when we will see face to face rather than in a mirror dimly. Fill me now with Your Holy Spirit as a means not only for loving You perfectly, but to empower me for the tasks I have upon this earth, for Jesus' sake. Amen.

— 5 —

POUR OUT YOUR HEART TO GOD

Prayer is a sincere, sensible, affectionate *pouring out of the heart or soul to God*, through Christ, in the strength and assistance of the Holy Spirit, for such things as God has promised, or according to the Word of God, for the good of the Church, with submission in faith to the will of God.

When you pray, you pour out your heart or soul to God. Prayer is an unbosoming of your self, an opening of your heart to God, an affectionate pouring out of your soul in requests, sighs, and groans. David says, "All my longings lie open before you, O Lord: my sighing is not hidden from you" (Psalm 38:9). And again:

My soul thirsts for God, for the living God.

When can I go and meet with God?. . .
These things I remember
as I pour out my soul:
how I used to go with the multitude,
leading the procession to the house of God,
with shouts of joy and thanksgiving
among the festive throng (Psalm 42:2,4).

Notice especially his words: "I pour out my soul." This expression signifies that in prayer you give your very life and whole strength to God. And in another place David declared, "Trust in him at all times, O people; pour out your hearts to him, for God is our refuge" (Psalm 62:8).

In this type of prayer God promises to deliver us, poor creatures, out of captivity: "But if from there you seek the Lord your God, you will find him if you look for him with all your heart and with all your soul" (Deuteronomy 4:29).

Prayer must be a pouring out of the heart or soul to God. This shows the excellency of the spirit of prayer. Prayer attends to the great God of the universe. Someone may ask, "When shall I come and appear before God?" We answer that the one who prays indeed to God, prays when he sees an emptiness in all things under heaven, when he realises that in God alone there is rest and satisfaction for the soul. Paul wrote: "The widow who is really in need and left all alone puts her hope in God and continues night and day to pray and to ask God for help" (1 Timothy 5:5). David expressed the very same sentiment:

In you, O Lord, I have taken refuge;
let me never be put to shame.
Rescue me and deliver me in your
    righteousness;
turn your ear to me and save me.
Be my rock of refuge,
to which I can always go;
give the command to save me,
for you are my rock and my fortress.
Deliver me, O my God, from the hand of the
    wicked,

from the grasp of evil and cruel men.
For you have been my hope, O Sovereign Lord,
my confidence since my youth (Psalm 71:1-5).

To pray rightly, you must make God your hope, stay and all. Right prayer sees nothing substantial and worth looking after except God. And that, as I said before, prayer does in a sincere, sensible and affectionate way.

PRAYER

O Lord, my enemies are encamped all about me, even my spiritual foes. They would have me sink again into the miry clay of sin and defeat. They would entice me to sin once again, or they would drive others to sin against me. Protect me, O my God. Send forth Your ministering angels to meet my needs. May they build a hedge about me so the darts of the evil one will not reach my heart. O Lord, I give my whole self to You. To whom can I turn if not to You, O God? You are my strength and my redeemer. I trust in You and I will not fear, for You are on Your Throne and I am ever before You through the atoning sacrifice of Jesus Christ. It is through Him that I offer my prayers to You, O God. Amen.

— 6

PRAYER THROUGH CHRIST

Prayer is a sincere, sensible, affectionate pouring out of the heart or soul to God, *through Christ*, in the strength and assistance of the Holy Spirit, for such things as God has promised, or according to the Word of God for the good of the Church, with submission in faith to the will of God.

We must add *through Christ* to every consideration of prayer in order to know whether or not it is true prayer, even though in appearance it may be eminent and eloquent.

Christ is the Way. Jesus Christ is the Person through whom we gain admittance into the presence of God. Without Christ, your desires will not come under the care of the God. The scriptures make this clear, for Jesus declared:

"I am the way and the truth and the life. No one comes to the Father except through me" (John 14:6). And further, note that Jesus also said, "And I will do whatever you ask in my name, so that the Son may bring glory to the Father. You may ask me for anything in my name, and I will do it" (John 14:13,14).

This was Daniel's way when he prayed for the people of God. He did it in the Name of Christ: "Now, our God, hear the prayers and petitions of your servant. For your sake, O Lord, look with favour on your desolate sanctuary" (Daniel 9:17). And we find the same with David: "For the sake of your name, O Lord," that is, Your Christ's sake, "forgive my iniquity, though it is great" (Psalm 25:11).[1]

Not everyone who mentions Christ's Name in prayer really and truly and effectually prays to God in the Name of Christ or through Him. The hardest part in prayer is coming to God through Christ. A person may be sensible of His works, and sincerely desire His mercy, and yet not be able to come to God by Christ. The person who comes to God by Christ must first have the knowledge of Him: "And without faith it is impossible to please God, because anyone who comes to him must believe that he exists and that he rewards those who earnestly seek him" (Hebrews 11:6). And so he who comes to God through Christ must be enabled to know Christ. "Lord," said Moses, "teach me your ways so I may know you and continue to find favour with you" (Exodus 33:13).

No one but the Father can truly reveal Jesus Christ to your soul: "All things have been committed to me by my Father. No one knows the Son except the Father, and no one knows the Father except the Son and those to whom the Son chooses to reveal him" (Matthew 11:27). To come to God through Christ means God has shrouded you under the shadow of the Lord Jesus, as a person is shrouded under a thing for safeguard. Hence, David so often terms Christ his shield, buckler, tower, fortress, and rock of defence (see Psalms 18, 27, and 28). David prays this way not only because he overcame his enemies by Christ, but because through Him he found favour with God the Father.

Likewise, God said to Abraham in a vision: "Do not be afraid Abram. I am your shield, your very great reward" (Genesis 15:1). The person, therefore, who comes to God through Christ must have faith, by which he puts his trust in Christ, so that he appears before God in Christ.

The person who has faith is born of God or born again, so he becomes one of the sons of God. By faith he is joined to Christ, and made a member of Him. "Jesus answered, 'I tell you the truth, no one can enter the kingdom of God unless he is born of water and the Spirit. Flesh gives birth to flesh, but the Spirit gives birth to spirit' " (John 3:5,6). Therefore, I say to you who are born again, as a member of Christ you can come to God. You can pray as a member of Christ, so that God looks upon you as a part of Christ, as a part of His body, His flesh and bones. You are united to Him by election, conversion, illumination, and the Holy Spirit having been conveyed into your heart by God: "for we are members of his body" (Ephesians 5:30).

So now, we can come to God in Christ's merits, in His blood, righteousness, victory and intercession. We can stand before God, being accepted in the One He loves (see Ephesians 1:6). Because you are a member of the Lord Jesus Christ, because you are under this consideration, you are admitted into the presence of God and can come before God in prayer. By virtue of this union with Christ, the Holy Spirit is given to abide in you. For this reason, you are able to pour out yourself before God in prayer, with His attention to your case and with His willingness to answer.

PRAYER

O Lord, I give You thanks that in all my prayers I do come to You through Jesus Christ, because His blood which He shed for my sins covers me and enables me to approach the Throne of Grace. May I more consciously recognise my need of Jesus in all that I do, and especially in my prayers. May I honour Him more as I seek to bring glory to You in all my requests. Teach me to pray for those things which will be for the good of your Church. Inspire me by Your Holy Spirit to pray for those people and things You would have me pray for, in the faith that You would hear me and want to answer my prayer through Jesus' Name and for His sake. Amen.

---

1. Some Bible scholars have taught (along with John Bunyan here) that David, Daniel, Moses and some of the other Old Testament saints knew Jesus Christ, the Son of God, in His pre-incarnate state (before He was born). Jesus probably taught this in Matthew 22:41-46:

> While the Pharisees were gathered together, Jesus asked them, "What do you think about the Christ? Whose son is he?" "The son of David," they replied. He said to them, "How is it then that David, speaking by the Spirit, calls him 'Lord'? For he says, "'The Lord said to my Lord: "Sit at my right hand until I put your enemies under your feet."' If then David calls him 'Lord', how can he be his son?" No one could say a word in reply, and from that day on no one dared to ask him any more questions.

    The implication from this verse is that David saw the Messiah, the Son of God, sitting at the right hand of God before He was born and that he prayed to Him as "Lord". He saw and heard God the Father say to God the Son,"Sit at my right hand." Jesus asks, since this is so, how can the Messiah also be the son of David? The scribes and the Pharisees did not want to admit the implication that Jesus Christ existed as the son of God before He was born of Mary, so they did not dare "ask him any more questions." See also Mark 12:36, Luke 20:42 and Peter's application of this passage in Acts 2:34. There are many Old Testament names, such as Shield, Buckler and Tower, that Christians have applied to Jesus Christ. For an extensive list of these names see *The Open Bible Edition — New American Standard Version*, (Nashville: Thomas Nelson Publishers, 1976, 1978), pages 88-90, or Charles G. Finney, *Principles of Union with Christ*, compiled and edited by L.G. Parkhurst, Jr. (Minneapolis: Bethany House Publishers, 1985), pages 149-154.

— 7

PRAYER IN THE HOLY SPIRIT

Prayer is a sincere, sensible, affectionate pouring out of the heart or soul to God, through Christ, *in the strength and assistance of the Holy Spirit*, for such things as God has promised, or according to the Word of God, for the good of the Church, with submission in faith to the will of God.

Praying through Christ, praying in union with Christ, and praying in the strength and assistance of the Holy Spirit, depend so much upon one another that you will find it impossible for your prayers to be *prayers* apart from this relationship. Though some prayers may be famous, apart from Christ and the Holy Spirit God rejects those prayers. For without a sincere, sensible, affectionate

41

pouring out of the heart to God, your prayer will only be lip-labour. If your prayers are not through Christ, they fall far short of ever sounding well in the ears of God.

So also, if your prayers are not in the strength and assistance of the Holy Spirit, you can be like the sons of Aaron, offering with strange fire. Remember this tragic affair:

> Aaron's sons Nadab and Abihu took their censers, put fire in them and added incense; and they offered unauthorised fire before the Lord, contrary to his command. So fire came out from the presence of the Lord and consumed them, and they died before the Lord. Moses then said to Aaron, "This is what the Lord spoke of when he said: Among those who approach me I will show myself holy; in the sight of all the people I will be honoured." Aaron remained silent. (Leviticus 10:1-3)

I shall speak more of this later. In the meantime, remember that those things which are not petitioned through the teaching and assistance of the Holy Spirit cannot possibly be according to the will of God.

Paul wrote to the Romans:

> In the same way, the Spirit helps us in our weakness. We do not know what we ought to pray for, but the Spirit himself intercedes for us with groans that words cannot express. And he who searches our hearts knows the mind of the Spirit, because the Spirit intercedes for the saints in accordance with God's will (Romans 8:26,27).

No person or church in the world can come to God in prayer except by the assistance of the Holy Spirit: "For through him we both have access to the Father by one Spirit" (Ephesians 2:18). Because these scriptures contain such a full revelation of the spirit of prayer, and of a person's inability to pray without the Holy Spirit's aid, I shall in a few words comment upon them.

"FOR WE." Consider first the person speaking, even Paul, and in his person all the apostles also speak. "We apostles, we extraordinary officers, we wise master-builders, some of whom have been caught up into paradise," they seem to be saying, "we know not what we should pray for," apart from the Holy Spirit's assistance (see Romans 15:16; 1 Corinthians 3:10; 2 Corinthians 12:4).

Surely no one will think that Paul and his companions were not as able to have done any work for God as any pastor, pope or proud prelate in the church. They could have written a *Common Prayer Book* as well as those who at first composed it. They were not a whit behind pope or prelate either in grace or gifts. But they chose not to write a *Prayer Book*. [1] But here now, the wise men of our days are so well skilled that they have both the manner and the matter of their prayers at their fingertips. They can set a certain prayer for each day, and write these for a day twenty years before it comes. They write one for Christmas, another for Easter, and others for the six days after that. They have also determined how many syllables must be said in every one of their prayers at their public exercises. For each saint's day, they have prayers ready for the generations yet unborn to say. All which the apostles came short of, "as not being able to compose in so profound a manner!"

"FOR WE DO NOT KNOW WHAT WE OUGHT TO PRAY." We know not the matter of the things for which we should pray, neither the objects for which we are to pray, nor the medium by or through whom we pray: none of these things we know, except by the help and assistance of the Holy Spirit. Should we pray for communion with God through Christ? Should we pray for faith, for justification by grace, and a truly sanctified heart? We know none of these things unless the Holy Spirit prompts us to pray for them. Scripture declares: "For who among men knows the thoughts of a man except the man's spirit within him? In the same way no one knows the thoughts of God except the Spirit of God" (1 Corinthians 2:11). Here alas! The Apostle speaks of inward and spiritual things which the world knows not.

PRAYER

Dear Father, in the Name of Jesus Christ, I pray that You will send Your Holy Spirit down upon me, anoint me, fill me, use me, teach me how to pray as I ought. Dear Father, in my own strength I am less than useless. Empower me, as I begin to obey You and do the tasks You have assigned me this day. Motivate me to pray beyond any written prayer to really express my deepest longings and need of You. I praise You for the Holy Spirit when He reveals any unconfessed sins that are blocking my path to deeper communion with You, and I thank You for my Saviour Jesus Christ Who is ready and willing to intercede for me. Help me to love much, and be gracious to all those who need my care, concern, and compassion through Jesus Christ. Amen.

---

1. At this time Bunyan was writing and fighting for the right of people to pray prayers other than those prepared and printed in the *Common Prayer Book*, and he was determined to teach those who knew no other method of prayer what Scripture teaches about how they could pray their own prayers to God. Bunyan was in prison at this time for preaching and praying his own prayers in public.

—— 8 ——

PRAYER AND THE WORD OF GOD

Prayer is a sincere, sensible, affectionate pouring out of the heart or soul to God, through Christ, in the strength and assistance of the Holy Spirit, *for such things as God has promised, or according to the Word of God,* for the good of the Church, with submission in faith to the will of God.

Jesus commanded:

> When you pray, go into your room, close the door and pray to your Father, who is unseen. Then your Father, who sees what is done in secret, will reward you. And when you pray, do not keep on babbling like pagans, for they

think they will be heard because of their many words. Do not be like them, for your Father knows what you need before you ask him (Matthew 6:6-8).

We pray, when we pray within the compass of God's Word; and it is blasphemy, or at best vain babbling, when the petition is contrary to the Bible. David, therefore, while in prayer, kept his eye on the Word of God. "I am laid low in the dust," he cried, "preserve my life according to your word. . .My soul is weary with sorrow; strengthen me according to your word" (Psalm 119:25,28). And indeed, the Holy Spirit does not immediately quicken and stir up the heart of the praying Christian without the Word, but only by, with, and through the Word. The Holy Spirit brings the Word to the heart, and opens the Word to us so that we are provoked to go to the Lord in prayer, and tell Him how it is with us, and also to argue and supplicate according to the Word.

This was the experience of Daniel, that mighty prophet of God. Daniel, understanding by the Word that the captivity of the children of Israel was near to an end, made his prayer to God according to the Scriptures:

> In the first year of Darius son of Xerxes (a Mede by descent), who was made ruler over the Babylonian kingdom—in the first year of his reign, I, Daniel, understood from the Scriptures, according to the word of the Lord given to Jeremiah the prophet, that the desolation of Jerusalem would last seventy years. So I turned to the Lord God and pleaded with him in prayer and petition, in fasting, and in sackcloth and ashes.
> (Daniel 9:1-3)

So I say, as the Spirit is the Helper and the Governor of the soul, when you pray according to the will of God, you should be guided by and pray according to the Word of God and His promises. Hence, our Lord Jesus Christ came to a stop in His prayer for deliverance, although His life lay at stake. He said that He could now pray to His Father, and that He could give Him twelve legions of angels; but how then would the Scriptures be fulfilled (see Matthew 26:53,54)? If there were but a word for it in the Scriptures, Jesus would have soon been out of the hands of His enemies and would have soon been helped by the angels; but the Scriptures would not warrant this type of praying because He was to die for our sins.

True prayer, then, must be according to the Word of God and His promises. The Spirit by the Word must direct both the manner and the matter of prayer. "So what shall I do?" asks Paul. "I will pray with my spirit, but I will also pray with my mind; I will sing with my spirit, but I will also sing with my mind" (1 Corinthians 14:15). [1] There is no understanding without the Word. For if people reject the Word of God, "what kind of wisdom do they have?" (Jeremiah 8:9).

PRAYER

Dear heavenly Father, even as Paul desired to speak sound words in prayer by the Holy Spirit's leading, so I pray that You would reveal to me the promises and words of Scripture that I may claim for my particular situations in life. I pray that You would guide me in the application of Your Word in prayer, so that I might pray in accordance with Your will and then be able to manifest Your glorious loving power to all for Jesus' sake. Amen.

---

1. Bunyan and many other Bible expositors have translated and interpreted this verse to read, "I will pray with the Spirit, but I will also pray with my mind." It is in this sense that Bunyan uses this verse in the context here and in other places.

9

PRAYER FOR THE CHURCH

> Prayer is a sincere, sensible, affectionate pouring out of the heart or soul to God, through Christ, in the strength and assistance of the Holy Spirit, for such things as God has promised, or according to the Word of God, *for the good of the Church*, with submission in faith to the will of God.

This clause, *for the good of the Church*, includes whatsoever tends to the honour of God, Christ's advancement, or His people's benefit. For God and Christ and His people are so linked together that if the good of one is prayed for, then the Church, the glory of God, and the advancement of Christ must all be included. For as Christ is in the Father, so the saints are in Christ, and when you pray for other Christians you touch the apple of God's eye; therefore, if you pray for the peace of Jerusalem, then you pray for what God requires of you. For Jerusalem will never be in perfect peace until she is in heaven; and Christ desires nothing more than to have her there. That also is the place that God through Christ has given her. He then who prays for the peace and good of Zion, or the Church, asks in prayer for that which Christ has purchased with His blood; and also that which the Father has given to Him as the price thereof.

Now he who prays for this, must pray for abundance of grace for the Church and for help against all her temptations; that God would let nothing be too hard for her; and that all things might work together for her good; that God would keep her blameless. The Scriptures have taught us to pray:

> To him who is able to keep you from falling and to present you before his glorious presence without fault and with great joy—to the only God our Saviour be glory, majesty, power and authority, through Jesus Christ our Lord, before all ages, now and for evermore! Amen (Jude 24,25).

We should pray for God to protect and defend the sons of God to His glory, in the midst of a crooked and perverse nation: this must be our daily prayer. And this is the substance of Christ's own prayer in the seventeenth chapter of John. All of Paul's prayers ran in the same way, as one of his prayers eminently shows:

> And this is my prayer: that your love may abound more and more in knowledge and depth of insight, so that you may be able to discern what is best and may be pure and blameless until the day of Christ, filled with the fruit of righteousness that comes through Jesus Christ—to the glory and praise of God (Philippians 1:9-11).

Paul's prayer was a short prayer, you see, and yet full of good desires for the Church, from the beginning to the end: that she may go on, and go on in the most excellent frame of spirit, without blame, sincere, and without offence, until the day of Christ, let her temptations or persecutions be what they will. [1]

PRAYER

Dear heavenly Father, I confess that many of my prayers are truly selfish, because I neglect to pray for the good of Your Church and the welfare of Your servants around the world. Too often, I simply believe that everything being done in the Church will get done by You without my prayers. I thank You for the great honour that You have bestowed upon all Christians, by making their prayers count for the good of Your Church and for the sanctification of believers. Please continue to inspire us by Your Spirit and Your Word so that we might know Your will for the church. May we be like Daniel praying for the return of the Israelites to Jerusalem. May we pray for those things You intend for Your Church on earth. In the Name of Your Son, Jesus Christ, I pray these things. Amen.

---

1. See especially Paul's own prayers and account of his prayers in Ephesians 1:16-20; 3:14-19; and Colossians 1:9-13.

—10—

PRAYING IN THE WILL OF GOD

Prayer is a sincere, sensible, affectionate pouring out of the heart or soul to God, through Christ, in the strength and assistance of the Holy Spirit, for such things as God has promised, or according to the Word of God, for the good of the Church, *with submission in faith to the will of God.*

True prayer submits to the will of God and says, "your will be done" (Matthew 6:10). Therefore, the people of the Lord in humility are to lay themselves and their prayers, and all that they have, at the foot of their God to be disposed of by Him as He in His heavenly wisdom sees best. Yet, when we lay our whole selves before Him, we do not doubt that God will answer our prayers in a way that shall be most for our advantage and His glory. When the saints of God, therefore, pray with submission to the will of God, they do not argue or doubt or question but trust in faith God's love and kindness to them. They recognise that they are not at all times wise, and that sometimes Satan may get the advantage over them, so to tempt them to pray for that which, if they had it, would neither prove to be for God's glory nor His people's best interest and good.

John wrote in his letters, "This is the confidence we have in approaching God: that if we ask anything according to his will, he hears us. And if we know that he hears us—whatever we ask—we know that we have what we asked of him" (1 John 5:14,15). For as I have said before, the petition that is not brought before God in and through the Holy Spirit will not be answered, because it is outside the will of God. For only the Holy Spirit knows how to pray according to the will of God:

> However, as it is written: "No eye has seen, no ear has heard, no mind has conceived what God has prepared for those who love him"—but God has revealed it to us by his Spirit. The Spirit searches all things, even the deep things of God. For who among men knows the thoughts of a man except the man's spirit within him? In the same way no one knows the thoughts of God except the Spirit of God (1 Corinthians 2:9-11).

Paul also writes to the Romans: "We do not know what we ought to pray for" (Romans 8:26). Now notice this: "what we ought to pray for"! If we do not think about this, or if we do not understand its meaning in the spirit and the truth of it, we may devise, as Jeroboam did, another way of worship both for matter and manner from what is revealed in the Word of God.

> Jeroboam thought to himself, "The kingdom is now likely to revert to the house of David. If these people go up to offer sacrifices at the temple of the Lord in Jerusalem, they will

again give their allegiance to their lord, Rehoboam king of Judah. They will kill me and return to King Rehoboam." After seeking advice, the king made two golden calves. He said to the people, "It is too much for you to go up to Jerusalem. Here are your gods, O Israel, who brought you up out of Egypt." One he set up at Bethel, and the other in Dan. And this thing became sin; the people went even as far as Dan to worship the one there (1 Kings 12:26-30).

Paul says that we must pray as we ought; and this *we* cannot do by all the art, skill, and cunning devices of men or angels. "We do not know what we ought to pray for, but the Spirit himself..."; no further, *it must be* "the Spirit himself" who helps us in our infirmities, not the Spirit and our lusts. What man of his own brain may imagine and devise is one thing, and what we are commanded and ought to do is another. Many ask and have not, because they ask amiss, and so are never any nearer enjoying those things they ask for: "When you ask, you do not receive, because you ask with wrong motives, that you may spend what you get on your pleasures" (James 4:3).

Praying at random apart from a prayer book will not put off God, nor will it cause Him to answer your prayer. While you are praying, God is searching your heart to see from what root and spirit your prayer arises. John wrote, "This is the confidence we have in approaching God: that if we ask anything according to his will, he hears us" (1 John 5:14). And again Paul wrote, "He who searches our hearts knows the mind of the Spirit, because the Spirit intercedes for the saints in accordance with God's will" (Romans 8:27). God answers only those requests that are according to His will, and nothing else. Only the Holy Spirit can teach us to pray according to His will. He is the only Being able to search out all things, even the deep things of God. Without the Holy Spirit, though we had a thousand common prayer books, we would not know what we ought to pray for, especially since we have infirmities which make us absolutely incapable of praying according to His will.

PRAYER

Come Holy Spirit, indwell my heart and soul and mind and spirit. Reveal to me the things of God's mind and will that I might pray according to what He has planned for me and for His Church. Guide me as I read the Scriptures that I might see the promises God has for me and for His Church, and teach me to pray and claim these promises in His behalf. Forgive me for my little faith, which too often fails to trust that You really are working in my best interests and for my good through Jesus Christ. Amen.

— 11 —————————————

THE SPIRIT OVERCOMES OUR WEAKNESSES

Without the Holy Spirit, we are so weak that we will not, with all other means whatsoever, think one right saving thought of God, of Christ, or of the blessings He has reserved for those who love Him. Therefore, the psalmist said of the wicked, "In his pride the wicked does not seek him; in all his thoughts there is no room for God" (Psalm 10:4).

The wicked might imagine God to be altogether such a being as they are themselves. Prior to the great flood, God looked upon the earth and, "The Lord saw how great man's wickedness on the earth had become, and that every inclination of the thoughts of his heart was only evil all the time" (Genesis 6:5). And when Noah sacrificed to God after the flood, "The Lord smelled the pleasing aroma and said in his heart: 'Never again will I curse the ground because of man, even though every inclination of his heart is evil from childhood.' " (Genesis 8:21).

Unless the Holy Spirit helps us in our weakness, we

cannot conceive rightly of God to Whom we pray, of Christ through Whom we pray, of the things for which we should pray, nor how we shall address God. The Holy Spirit is the Revealer of things to us and He gives us understanding of them; therefore, Christ told His disciples, when He promised to send the Holy Spirit, the Comforter: "He will bring glory to me by taking from what is mine and making it known to you" (John 16:14). It is as though He said, "I know you are naturally dark and ignorant with regard to understanding any of my things; though you try this course and the other, your ignorance will still remain; the veil is spread over your heart, and only the Holy Spirit can take away that veil and give you spiritual understanding."

Right prayer must be made both in the outward expression and the inward intention: it must come from what the soul apprehends in the light of the Holy Spirit. Otherwise, the prayer will be condemned as vain and an abomination, because the heart and tongue do not go along jointly in the same intention, neither indeed will they unless the Spirit helps our infirmities and weaknesses. And this David knew full well when he cried, "O Lord, open my lips, and my mouth will declare your praise" (Psalm 51:15). I suppose that most can imagine that David could speak and express himself as well as others, as well as any in our generation, as is clearly manifested by his words and by his works. Nevertheless, when this good man, this prophet, went into God's worship, the Lord had to help him. He knew he could do nothing by himself, so he prayed, "O Lord, open my lips, and my mouth will declare your praise" (Psalm 51:15). He could not speak one right word, unless the Holy Spirit gave him proper expression. Remember that Paul writes clearly, "The Spirit helps us in our weakness. We do not know what we ought to pray for, but the Spirit himself intercedes for us with groans that words cannot express" (Romans 8:26).

PRAYER

O Lord God, I thank You for the blessing of Your Word and Spirit, for by Your Word I can know many of the deep things of You, and by Your Spirit I can understand and apply these deep things to my life and in my conversations with others. Only too well do I recognise my weakness and my inability to know or do any good thing apart from You, and I thank You for Your Spirit Who is an ever present help in any time of weakness or trouble. Please continue to lead me in the paths of righteousness for Your Name's sake. Amen.

—12

THE SPIRIT AND EFFECTIVE PRAYER

To pray effectively, we must pray with the Holy Spirit, because without the Holy Spirit we are foolish, hypocritical, cold and unseemly in our prayers. Without the assistance of the Holy Spirit, our prayers are deplorable to God. Jesus declared: "Woe to you, teachers of the Law and Pharisees, you hypocrites! You devour widows' houses and for a show make lengthy prayers. Therefore you will be punished more severely" (Matthew 23:14).

God does not regard the quality of our voice, nor the seeming earnestness and affection of our praying, if the Holy Spirit is not aiding us in our prayers. Without the guidance of the Holy Spirit, man, as man, is so full of wickedness, that he will not keep a word, a thought or a prayer clean and acceptable to God through Christ. For this reason, the Pharisees, with all their prayers, were rejected. The Pharisees distinguished themselves with their many words. They were noted for length of time spent in prayer, but they did not have the Holy Spirit to help them; so, they prayed only with their infirmities and weaknesses. They fell far short of a sincere, sensible, affectionate pouring out of their souls to God, through the strength of the Holy Spirit.

The prayers that ascend to heaven are the prayers that are sent there by the Holy Spirit: only this prayer is effective.

Only the Holy Spirit can show a person clearly his misery by nature, and so put him into a posture of prayer. Talk is but talk, as we used to say, and so it is only mouth-worship. There must be a sense of misery in sin. O the cursed hypocrisy that is in most hearts, and that accompanies many thousands of praying people! But now the Spirit will sweetly show a person his misery, where he is in his spiritual growth, and what is likely to become of him apart from Christ. The Holy Spirit will also show the intolerableness of our condition apart from faith in the Saviour. The Holy Spirit effectually convinces of sin and misery if we are without the Lord Jesus, and so puts us into a sweet, serious, sensible, affectionate way of praying to God according to His Word. Jesus promised:

> But I tell you the truth: It is for your own good that I am going away. Unless I go away, the Counsellor will not come to you; but if I go, I will send him to you. When he comes, he will convict the world of guilt in regard to sin and righteousness and judgment; in regard to sin, because men do not believe in me; in regard to righteousness, because I am going to the Father, where you can see me no longer; and in regard to judgment, because the prince of this world now stands condemned (John 16:7-11).

Even if people did see their sins, without the help of the Holy Spirit they would not pray. For they would run away from God and utterly despair of mercy. This happened to Adam and Eve, Cain, and Judas. When a person is indeed sensible of his sin and God's curse, then it is a difficult thing to persuade him to pray. Apart from the influence of the Holy Spirit, a sinner will say, "It's no use.

We will continue with our own plans; each of us will follow the stubbornness of his evil heart" (Jeremiah 18:12). A sinner has often concluded, "I am so vile, so wretched, and so cursed a creature, that I shall never be regarded by God!" The Holy Spirit comes and stays the soul. He helps a person hold up his face to God by letting into his heart some small sense of mercy to encourage him to go to God. For this reason the Spirit is called "the Comforter".

PRAYER

Dear heavenly Father, forgive me for being so blind to Your work in my life. I confess that I have not glorified You, and I have not recognised fully the wonderful work of Your Holy Spirit in my life. Forgive me for not acknowledging You to be the loving and gracious God that You are, and then failing to thank You for leading me out of the darkness and into the light by Your Spirit, even when I was predisposed to live my own life without regard to You or Your concerns. May I now seek to honour You by sharing with others the good news of how You work in our lives, even while we are yet sinners, that we might learn to pray through the Holy Spirit. Amen.

—13—

THE RIGHT WAY TO PRAY

No one can know how to come to God the right way unless he learns how to pray in or with the Holy Spirit. People may easily say that they come to God in His Son, but it is the hardest thing for them to come to God the right way and in His own way without the Holy Spirit.

The Holy Spirit must show us the way to come to God, and also what there is in God that makes Him so desirable. Moses prayed, "If you are pleased with me, teach me your ways so I may know you and continue to find favour with you" (Exodus 33:13). Jesus taught that the Holy Spirit "will bring glory to me by taking from what is mine and making it known to you" (John 16:14).

Even if you saw your misery and sin, and the way to come to God through Jesus Christ, without the Holy Spirit you would never claim a share in God, Christ, or mercy. O how great a task for the poor soul who becomes sensible of his sin and the wrath of God to say in faith this one word:

"Father!" I tell you the difficulty is in this very thing: when a person is aware of his sin, he is *afraid* to call God "Father". "Oh!" says the sinner, "I dare not call Him 'Father'!" Therefore, the Holy Spirit must be sent into the hearts of God's people for this very thing, to cry "Father". It is too great a thing and too great a work for anyone to knowingly and believingly call God "Father": he must have the Holy Spirit's aid.

When I say "knowingly" call upon God as Father, I mean, "knowing what it is to be a child of God and to be born again". And when I say "believingly" call God Father, I mean, "for the soul to believe, and that from good experience, that the work of grace is wrought in him". This is the right way to call upon God as "Father". Not as many knowingly and believingly call God "Father" as say the Lord's Prayer from memory.

Here is the life of prayer: when in or with the Holy Spirit a person who has been made sensible of his sin, and of how to come to the Lord for mercy, comes and says in the strength of the Holy Spirit, "Father". That one word spoken in faith is better than a thousand "prayers", as men call them, that are written and read, in a formal, cold, and lukewarm way. Paul wrote to encourage Christians with this central truth: "Because you are sons, God sent the Holy Spirit of his Son into our hearts, the Spirit who calls out, '*Abba*, Father' " (Galatians 4:6).

Oh, how far short are those who count it enough to teach themselves and their children to say the Lord's Prayer, the creeds, the other sayings; when as God knows, they are senseless of themselves, their misery in sin, or of what it is to be brought to God through Christ! Ah poor soul! Study your misery! Cry to God to show you your confused blindness and ignorance, before you begin to call God your Father or teach your children to do so. Know that to say God is your Father in a way of prayer or conversation, without any experience of the work of grace in your soul, is to say you are a Christian when you are not, and so you lie! You say, "Our Father", and God says, "You blaspheme!" You say that you are a true Christian, but God says, "You lie!"

Our risen Lord told the Church in Smyrna: "These are the words of him who is the First and the Last, who died and came to life again. I know your afflictions and your poverty—yet you are rich! I know the slander of those who say they are Jews and are not, but are a synagogue of Satan" (Revelation 2:8,9). And He told the Church in Philadelphia: "I will make those who are of the synagogue of Satan, who claim to be Jews though they are not, but are liars—I will make them come and fall down at your feet and acknowledge that I have loved you" (Revelation 3:9).

And so much the greater is the sin when the sinner boasts of his pretended sanctity, as the Jews did to Christ in the eighth chapter of the Gospel of John, which then made Christ, even in plain terms tell them their doom for all their hypocritical pretences:

> "Abraham is our father," they answered.
>
> "If you were Abraham's children," said Jesus, "then you would do the things Abraham did. As it is, you are determined to kill me, a man who has told you the truth that I heard from God. Abraham did not do such things. You are doing the things your own father does."
>
> "We are not illegitimate children," they protested. "The only Father we have is God himself."
>
> Jesus said to them, "If God were your Father, you would love me, for I came from God and now am here. I have not come on my own; but he sent me. Why is my language not clear to you? Because you are unable to hear what I say. You belong to your father, the devil, and you want to carry out your father's desire. He was a murderer from the beginning, not holding to the truth, for there is no truth in him. When he lies, he speaks his native language, for he is a liar and the father of lies. Yet because I tell the truth, you do not believe me! Can any of you prove me guilty of sin? If I am telling the truth, why don't you believe me? He who belongs to God hears what God says. The

67

reason you do not hear is that you do not belong to God" (John 8:39-47).

PRAYER

Oh Father! Forgive me for all the times I have taken for granted the blessed opportunity to call You "Abba", Father. Since I have been adopted by You through faith in Your Son Jesus Christ as my Lord and Saviour, You have given me the privilege of coming to You as Your little child. But I confess that I have sometimes come to You childishly without counting my blessings and also the great price You paid so I could call You "Father". Please continue to bestow upon me the workings of Your grace for Jesus' sake. Amen.

— 14 —————————————

TO PRAY THE LORD'S PRAYER

Do you love to say the Lord's Prayer: "Our Father in heaven..." (Matthew 6:9)? Do you know the meaning of the very first words of this prayer? Can you indeed, with other Christians, cry, "Our Father"? Are you truly born again? Have you received the Spirit of adoption? Do you see yourself in Christ, and can you come to God as a member in Him? Or are you ignorant of these things, but still dare to say, "Our Father"? Is the devil really your father? Are you a desperate persecutor of the children of God? Have you cursed them in your heart many times?

Just because Christians are commanded to pray, "Our Father", all the blind, ignorant, sinful rabble in the world feel they must use the same words, "Our Father", too. And do you pray, "Hallowed be Thy Name", with all your heart? Do you study, by all honest and lawful ways, to advance the Name, Holiness, and Majesty of God? Does your heart and conversation agree with these words? Do you strive to imitate Christ in all the works of righteousness which God commands of you and prompts you to do? It is so, if you are one who can truly cry with God's permission, "Our Father".

Or is the imitation of Christ one of the least of your thoughts all the day so that you are a cursed hypocrite? Would you have the kingdom of God come indeed, and also His will to be done on earth as it is in heaven? Or would the sound of His trumpet make you run mad, afraid to see the rising of the dead, and afraid to reckon for all of the deeds you have done in the body? Are all the very thoughts of it altogether displeasing to you? If God's will were to be done on the earth, would it be to your ruin? There is never in heaven a rebel against God. If you are a rebel on earth, you must whirl down to hell.

Think of the other petitions in the Lord's Prayer. How sadly would those men look, and with what terror would they walk up and down the world, if they only knew the lying and blaspheming that proceeds out of their mouths even in their most pretended sanctity! May the Lord awaken you and teach your poor soul, in all humility, to take heed lest you be rash and unadvised with your heart, and much more with your mouth!

When you appear before God, as the wise man said, "Do not be quick with your mouth, do not be hasty in your heart to utter anything before God. God is in heaven and you are on earth, so let your words be few" (Ecclesiastes 5:2). Especially so, when you call God "Father" without some blessed experience and assurance of being born again when you come before Him.

PRAYER

O Father! I know that I have repeated the Lord's Prayer, perhaps thousands of times, without any real thought of what I was praying. I am conscious that I am a Christian, a born-again believer, who has every right to call You "Father", but I am aware and I confess that I have taken this privilege too lightly. I confess that there have been many times when if Your will had been done and Your kingdom come, as I had prayed, many of my plans and ways of living would have been radically disrupted. Help me in the

70

future, as Your Spirit guides me and prompts me, to really pray the Lord's Prayer from my heart. Lead me to pray expectantly and anxiously for that prayer to be answered in my life now as well as when You come again. Through the Name of Your Son, Jesus, I offer this prayer. Amen.

—15—

LIFT UP YOUR HEART TO GOD

True prayer, accepted by God, must be praying with the Holy Spirit, because only the Holy Spirit can lift up the soul or heart to God in prayer: "To man belong the plans of the heart, but from the Lord comes the reply of the tongue. All a man's ways seem innocent to him, but motives are weighed by the Lord. Commit to the Lord whatever you do, and your plans will succeed" (Proverbs 16:1-3). That is, in every work for God, and especially in prayer, if the heart runs with the tongue it must be prepared by the Spirit of God. Indeed, of itself, the tongue is very apt to run without either fear or wisdom; but when the tongue is the answer of the heart, and such a heart as is prepared by the Holy Spirit, then it speaks so as God commands and desires.

Remember the mighty words of David when he said that he lifted his heart and soul to God: "To you, O Lord, I lift up my soul; in you I trust, O my God" (Psalm 25:1). It is a great work for anyone without the strength of the Spirit to lift his heart and soul to God; therefore, I conceive that this is one of the great reasons why the Spirit of God is called the Spirit of supplication: "And I will pour out on the house of David and the inhabitants of Jerusalem a spirit of grace and supplication" (Zechariah 12:10). The Holy Spirit helps the heart when it makes its supplication; therefore, Paul wrote, "And pray in the Spirit on all occasions with all kinds of prayers and requests (supplications)" (Ephesians 6:18). And so also in the text we have been considering, "I will pray with the Spirit." Without your heart in it, prayer is like a sound without a life; and a heart will never pray to God unless it is lifted up by the Holy Spirit.

PRAYER

I thank You, Father, for the gift of Your Holy Spirit, for the gift of the Holy Scriptures, and for the gift of grace to Your servants, such as John Bunyan, so that Your will might be opened to me and to many others as well. I praise You for shining Your revealing light upon Bunyan while he was in the dark confines of his prison cell. I thank You for opening up to him the many Scriptures he has used in his studies of prayer and the Christian life. And I praise You and thank You further that even though Bunyan has passed from this world to the next, still he speaks! Inspire me, I pray, so I might do for others what You have done for me through others. In Jesus' Name. Amen.

— 16 —

HOW TO REST IN GOD

Your heart must be *lifted up* by the Holy Spirit, if you are to pray rightly. And when it is up, if you are to continue to pray rightly, your heart must be *held up* by the Holy Spirit. I do not know what or how it is with others, whether their hearts are lifted up by the Spirit of God and continued so or not, but there are some things I am sure of.

First, it is impossible for any manmade prayer book to lift up or prepare the heart to pray to God: that is the work of our great God Himself.

Second, prayer books are far from able to keep their hearts up when they are up. And indeed, here is the life of prayer: to have your heart kept with God in the duty of prayer. If it was a great matter for Moses to keep his hands lifted up to God in prayer, how much more then for us to keep our hearts lifted up to God (see Exodus 17:12).

God complains of the lack of keeping the heart at rest with Him in prayer. People draw near to Him with their mouth, and honour Him with their lips, but their hearts are far from Him: "The Lord says: 'These people come near to me with their mouth and honour me with their lips, but their hearts are far from me. Their worship of me is made up only of rules taught by men" (Isaiah 29:13). In Matthew 15:7-9, Jesus called the people who pray in this way, "hypocrites".

And truly, may I speak of my own experience, and tell you the difficulty of praying to God as I ought? It is enough to make poor, blind, carnal men entertain strange thoughts of me. For, as for my heart, when I go to pray, I find it is disinclined to go to God; and when it is with Him, so disinclined to stay with Him, that many times I am forced in my prayers; first, to beg God to take my heart and set it upon Himself in Christ; and second, when it is there, that He would keep it there. Many times I know not what to pray for, I am so blind. At other times I know not how to pray, I am so ignorant. Only, blessed by grace, the Holy Spirit helps us in our weakness: "Teach me your way, O Lord, and I will walk in your truth; give me an undivided heart, that I may fear your name. I will praise you, O Lord my God, with all my heart; I will glorify your name for ever" (Psalm 86:11,12).

Our heart faces many difficulties in the time of prayer. No one knows how many by-ways and back-lanes our heart may use to slip away from the presence of God. How much pride the heart has, if enabled with expressive language to pray to Him. How much hypocrisy, if praying before others. And how little conscience is there made of prayer between God and the soul in secret, unless the Spirit of supplication is there to help. When the Holy Spirit gets into the heart, then there is prayer indeed, and not until then.

PRAYER

O Lord God, I am too quickly learning that I can do nothing apart from Your Holy Spirit. Your Spirit lifts me up in prayer. Your Spirit prepares my heart for prayer. Your Spirit aids me in resting my heart and mind in You in prayer. Your Spirit prompts me to pray for the things of Your heart, and He leads me beyond selfish desires. May I be continually inspired by Your Spirit to say and do and pray consistently, that my life might be a witness to others regarding the blessed power of prayer and Your work through Your Spirit. Amen.

—17—

PRAYING WITH GROANS AND SIGHS

If you are to pray rightly, you must pray in and with the help and strength of the Holy Spirit, because you cannot possibly express yourself in prayer without Him. When I say, it is impossible for a person to express himself in prayer without the Holy Spirit, I mean, that it is impossible for the heart in a sincere and sensible affectionate way to pour itself out before God with those groans and sighs that come from a truly praying heart.

Your mouth and many words are not the main things to be looked to in prayer, but whether or not your heart is so full of affection and earnestness in prayer with God that it is impossible to express its sense and desire in words. When your desires are so strong and mighty that all the tears, groans, and words that can come from your heart cannot be uttered, then "the Spirit helps us in our weakness. We do not know what we ought to pray for, but the Spirit himself intercedes for us with groans that words cannot express" (Romans 8:26).

A poor prayer is just so many words. A person who *truly* prays one prayer shall after that never be able to express with his mouth or pen the unutterable desires, sense, affection, and longing that went to God in that prayer.

The best prayers often have more groans than words; and those with words are but a lean and shallow representation of the heart, life and spirit of prayer. In the Bible, you will not find any words of prayer in the mouth of Moses when he was going out of Egypt and was followed by Pharaoh. Yet, he made heaven ring again with his cry for: "the Lord said to Moses, 'Why are you crying out to me? Tell the Israelites to move on' " (Exodus 14:15). Moses expressed the inexpressible and unsearchable groans and cryings of his soul in and with the Holy Spirit. God is the God of spirits, and His eyes look further than at the outside of any duty whatsoever: "Moses and Aaron fell face down and cried out, "O God, God of the spirits of all mankind, will you be angry with the entire assembly when only one man sins?" (Numbers 16:22). I doubt that this is thought of by most of those who would be looked upon as a praying people.

The nearer a person comes to fulfilling any work that God has commanded him to do according to His will, the more hard and difficult it is; because man as man alone is not able to do it: he must have the aid of the Holy Spirit. Now prayer is not only a duty, but one of the most eminent of duties; therefore, so much the more difficult. Therefore, Paul knew what he said, "I will pray with the Spirit." He knew well that it was not what others wrote or said that could make him a praying person; nothing less than the Holy Spirit could do it.

PRAYER

O Lord, I do groan and sigh when I think of the immense tasks and responsibilities You have laid upon my shoulders. I groan and sigh because I know too well my failings and inadequacies. I groan and sigh, but I take hope in the promise that in my groans and confessions I am strengthened and forgiven and I am empowered and prayed for by Your Spirit. I groan and I sigh, but I know full well that Your burden is easy and Your yoke is light compared to my trying to live and work without You. I praise You that I have experienced the difference between slavery in fear and service in friendship with You. May I never forget my need of Your Spirit each moment of my life, and when I am groaning and sighing may I be encouraged with the knowledge that You are there praying with me and for me through Jesus Christ my Saviour. Amen.

—18—

PRAY WITHOUT FAINTING

True prayer must be with the Holy Spirit, or else you will fail in the very act of prayer itself; you will faint in the prosecution of the work. Prayer is an ordinance of God that must continue with a person as long as he is on this side of glory. But as I said before, it is not possible for a person to get up his heart to God in prayer, nor keep it there, without the assistance of the Holy Spirit. And if so, then for you to continue from time to time in prayer with God, you must be with the Spirit.

Christ tells us that people ought always to pray and not faint: "Jesus told his disciples a parable to show them that they should always pray and not give up" (Luke 18:1). And again, the Scriptures tell us that this is one definition of a hypocrite, that either he will not continue in prayer, or else if he does, his prayer will not be in the power, that is in the spirit of prayer, but in the form, for a pretence only: "Will he find delight in the Almighty? Will he call upon God at all times?" (Job 27:10). For this fault, among others, Jesus declared that hypocrites would suffer many woes (see Matthew 23).

It is easy for a hundred to fall from the power of prayer to its mere formality, and it is the hardest thing to keep on any one duty, especially prayer. Prayer is such a duty and work that a person without the help of the Spirit cannot so much as pray once, much less continue, without Him. The Holy Spirit inspires in us a sweet praying frame of mind; and in praying, He helps us so to pray as to have our prayers ascend into the ears of the Lord God of the Sabbath.

Jacob did not only begin his prayer, but he held to it: "I will not let you go unless you bless me" (Genesis 32:26). This is so of the godly:

> He struggled with the angel and overcame him; he wept and begged for his favour. He found him at Bethel and talked with him there—the Lord God Almighty, the Lord is his name of renown! But you must return to your God; maintain love and justice, and wait for your God always (Hosea 12:4-6).

But this could not be without the Spirit in prayer. It is through the Spirit that we have access to the Father: "For through him we both have access to the Father by one Spirit" (Ephesians 2:18).

The same thing is found in a remarkable place in Jude, when he stirred up the saints by the judgment of God upon the wicked to pray, to stand fast and continue to hold out in the faith of the gospel. Prayer was an excellent means for holding on to faith, without which he knew they would never be able to do it. Jude wrote: "But you, dear friends, build yourselves up in your most holy faith and pray in the Holy Spirit" (Jude 20). As if he had said, "Brethren, as eternal life is laid up for the people who hold out only, so you cannot hold out unless you continue praying in the Holy Spirit." The devil and the antichrist cheat and delude the world by keeping people in the formality of any duty apart from the Spirit; they will keep them in the formality of preaching, of hearing, of praying, etc. These are the ones who have a form of godliness, but deny its power and turn away (see 2 Timothy 3:5).

PRAYER

O Holy Father, send Your Holy Spirit and fill me again with the power of prayer and service. Empower me to keep on keeping on when exhaustion or even the cares of this world would pull me away from my time of communion with You. May I be certain that salvation rests only in You, and that I can bring the gospel to others in word and deed only if You are with me strengthening me so that the work is really Your work and not mine. May I be certain of these things in my mind, that I might truly stay with You in faith with my whole heart and soul, through Jesus Christ our Lord, Amen.

—19—

PRAY IN SPIRIT AND MIND

What is it to pray with the spirit and to pray with the understanding also? The Apostle Paul puts a clear distinction between praying with the spirit, and praying with the spirit and the understanding also. Therefore he wrote that he would "pray with the spirit", but then he added, "and I will pray with the understanding, ALSO." Paul made this distinction because the Corinthians were not observing that it was their duty to pray to the edification of themselves and others too: they were praying for their own commendation. So I judge: for many of them having extraordinary gifts, as to speak in different tongues, etc., were more for those mighty gifts than they were for the edifying of their brethren. This made Paul write to them, to let them understand that though extraordinary gifts were excellent, yet to do what they did to the edification of the Church was more excellent. Said the Apostle:

> For if I pray in a tongue, my spirit prays, but
> my mind is unfruitful. So what shall I do? I

will pray with my spirit, but I will also pray
with my mind; I will sing with my spirit, but
I will also sing with my mind. . .But in
the church I would rather speak five
intelligible words to instruct others than ten
thousand words in a tongue.
(1 Corinthians 14:14,15,19)

It is expedient then that the understanding should
be occupied in prayer, as well as the heart and mouth. That
which is done with understanding is done more effectually,
sensibly and heartily than that which is done without it.
This truth made the Apostle pray for the Colossians that
God would fill them with, "the knowledge of his will
through all spiritual wisdom and understanding"
(Colossians 1:9). And for the Ephesians he prayed that God
would give to them, "the Spirit of wisdom and revelation, so
that you may know him better" (Ephesians 1:17). He prayed
for the Philippians that God would make them abound,
"more and more in knowledge and depth of insight, so that
you may be able to discern what is best and may be pure
and blameless until the day of Christ, filled with the fruit of
righteousness that comes through Jesus Christ—to the glory
and praise of God" (Philippians 1:9-11).

A suitable understanding is good in everything a
person undertakes, either civil or spiritual; therefore, it must
be desired by all who would be praying people. In the
following pages, I will show you what it is to pray with the
understanding and I will do this experimentally. For the
making of right prayers, it is required that there should be a
good or spiritual understanding in all those who pray to
God.

To pray with understanding is to pray while being
instructed by the Holy Spirit in the understanding regarding
those things for which you are to pray. Though you are in
much need of pardon for sin and deliverance from the wrath
to come, if you do not understand this, you will either not
desire these things or else you will be so cold and lukewarm
in your desires after them that God will loathe your asking
for them. Thus it was with the church of Laodicea. They
lacked knowledge or spiritual understanding; they did not

know that they were so poor, wretched, blind and naked. Their lack of spiritual understanding made them and all their services so loathsome to Christ that He threatened to spew them out of His mouth (see Revelation 3:16,17).

Men without understanding may say the same words in prayer as others do, but if there is understanding in one and none in the other, there is, O there is a mighty difference, in speaking the very same words! The one speaking from a spiritual understanding of those things that he in words desires will know far more, in the receiving or in the denying of his desires, than the other who prays in words only without the understanding.

Spiritual understanding should see in the heart of God a readiness and a willingness to give those things to the soul that the soul really needs. By spiritual understanding, David could guess at the very thoughts of God towards him. And thus it was with the woman of Canaan: she did by faith and a right understanding discern, beyond all the rough bearing of Christ, a tenderness and willingness in His heart to save, which caused her to be vehement and earnest, yea, restless, until she did enjoy the mercy she needed (see Matthew 15:22-28).

Spiritual understanding, understanding the willingness in the heart of God to save sinners, will press the soul to seek after God and to cry for pardon. If a man should see a pearl worth a hundred pounds lying in a ditch and not understand the value of it, he would lightly pass it by. But if he once got knowledge of its value, he would venture up to the neck to get it. So it is with souls concerning the things of God. If a man once gets an understanding of the worth of them, then his heart, the very strength of his soul, runs after them: and he will never stop crying for them until he has them. The two blind men in the gospel, because they did certainly know that Jesus, who was going by them, was both able and willing to heal such infirmities as they were afflicted with, cried out; and the more they were rebuked, the more they cried out until He heard and answered their needs (see Matthew 20:29-31).

PRAYER

O Father, too often I lack spiritual discernment and I am not even aware of it! I do not understand the needs of my soul. Too often, I blunder on in prayer, requesting things I do not need or things that would hurt me or others. Help me to pray from an understanding heart that does not just mouth words. Help me to perceive Your answers to prayer when they are given or when my requests are denied for good reasons. Inspire me to praise You for all things, and thank You for both Your gifts and Your denials of my requests. Enlighten my mind by the special influence of Your Spirit to see the signs of the times and then pray for exactly what You are seeking to do for me and for others in answer to heartfelt prayers. I pray these things in the Name of Jesus, Who came to bring Truth into the world and be the Way to You. Amen.

—20

REASON WITH GOD

The enlightened understanding will see largeness enough in the promises of God from Scripture to encourage a person to pray. The understanding adds to God's promises so that a person can pray from strength to strength. It is a great encouragement to know what promises God has made to His people, so that His people can come and ask for them.

When your understanding is enlightened, you can come to God with suitable arguments or reasons regarding why He should answer your requests. Jacob reasoned with God in prayer on the basis of His promise to him:

> Then Jacob prayed, "O God of my father Abraham, God of my father Isaac, O Lord, who said to me, 'Go back to your country and your relatives, and I will make you prosper,' I am unworthy of all the kindness and faithfulness You have shown your servant. I had only my staff when I crossed

this Jordan, but now I have become two groups. Save me, I pray, from the hand of my brother Esau, for I am afraid he will come and attack me, and also the mothers with their children. But you have said, 'I will surely make you prosper and will make your descendants like the sand of the sea, which cannot be counted'." (Genesis 32:9-12)

Sometimes in a prayer of supplication, yet not in a verbal prayer only but even from the heart, the Holy Spirit will force through the understanding such effectual arguments that you will move the heart of God.

When Ephraim got a right understanding of his unseemly conduct towards the Lord, then he began to bemoan himself. In bemoaning himself, he used such arguments with the Lord that it affected His heart, drew out His forgiveness, and made Ephraim pleasant in His eyes through Jesus Christ our Lord. God declared through His prophet Jeremiah:

I have surely heard Ephraim's moaning: "You disciplined me like an unruly calf, and I have been disciplined. Restore me, and I will return, because you are the Lord my God. After I strayed, I repented; after I came to understand, I beat my breast. I was ashamed and humiliated because I bore the disgrace of my youth." Is not Ephraim my dear son, the child in whom I delight? Though I often speak against him, I still remember him. Therefore my heart yearns for him; I have great compassion for him. (Jeremiah 31:18-20)

Thus you see, just as it is required to pray with the Spirit, so it is required to pray with the understanding also.

To illustrate what has just been said, suppose that two beggars come to your door. One of them is indeed a poor, lame, wounded and starved creature; and the other is a healthy and lusty person. These two use the same words

92

in their begging: the one says that he is almost starved and so does the other. But the one who is indeed poor, lame, wounded and almost starved speaks with more sense, great feeling, and more of an understanding of what is mentioned in their begging than does the other one. You are able to discover the lame one by his more affectionate speaking and his bemoaning himself. His pain and poverty make him speak more in a spirit of lamentation than the other, and he shall be pitied sooner than the other by all those who have the least dram of natural affection or pity. Thus it is with God: there are some who out of custom and formality go and pray; there are others who go in the bitterness of their spirits. The one prays out of bare notion and naked knowledge; the other has his words forced from him by the anguish of his soul. Surely the latter is the one that God will look at and listen to, even to the one who is poor, the one who has a humble and contrite spirit before the Lord, the one who hears and understands His Word and trembles: "This is the one I esteem: he who is humble and contrite in spirit, and trembles at my word" (Isaiah 66:2).

PRAYER

Dear heavenly Father, help me to understand myself when I come to You in prayer. Help me to understand Your Word and the promises You have made to all Christians. Search me, O Lord, and show me my heart and deepest longings, reveal to me the exact nature of my wrongs. May Your Holy Spirit empower me to truly open myself before You with honesty that I might confess my sins and find forgiveness through faith in Jesus Christ and His redeeming work. You have promised, O God, that if I will confess my sins, then You will be faithful and just and forgive me for all my sins. I claim that promise for my life, and I pray that Your Holy Spirit would apply the assurance of Your forgiveness to my heart and understanding, for Jesus' sake. Amen.

— 21

THE MANNER OF PRAYER

A well-enlightened understanding is of admirable use in regard to the manner and matter of prayer. He that has his understanding well exercised to discern between good and evil, and a sense either of the misery of man or the mercy of God, does not need the writings of other men to teach him prayer by forms. Just as the person who feels pain does not need to be taught to cry, "Oh!" even so the person who has his understanding opened by the Holy Spirit does not need to be taught by other men's prayers, so that he cannot pray without them. The present sense, feeling, and pressure that lies upon his spirit provokes him to groan out his request unto the Lord.

When David had the pains of hell catching hold of him, and the sorrows of hell compassing about him, he did not need a bishop in a surplice to teach him to say, "O Lord save me!" He said:

The cords of death entangled me,

the anguish of the grave came upon me;
I was overcome by trouble and sorrow.
Then I called on the name of the Lord:
"O Lord, save me!"
The Lord is gracious and righteous;
our God is full of compassion.
The Lord protects the simple-hearted;
when I was in great need, he saved me.
(Psalm 116:3-6)

David didn't look into a book to teach him a certain form to use to pour out his heart before God. It is the nature of the heart of sick men, in their pain and sickness, to vent themselves for ease by dolorous groans and complainings to those who stand by them. The same was true of David in Psalm 38: "O Lord, do not forsake me; be not far from me, O my God. Come quickly to help me, O Lord my Saviour" (Psalm 38:21,22). And thus, blessed be the Lord, it is the same with all those who are endued with the grace of God.

It is necessary for you to have an enlightened understanding, so you may be kept in the continuation of the duty of prayer.

The people of God are not ignorant of how many wiles, tricks and temptations the devil has to make upon a poor soul, who is truly willing to have the Lord Jesus Christ as his Saviour, and that upon Christ's terms too. The devil tempts that soul to be weary of seeking the face of God, and to think that God is not willing to have mercy on such a one as he. "Ay," says Satan, "you may pray indeed, but you shall not prevail. You see your heart is hard, cold, dull and dead. You do not pray with the Spirit. You do not pray in good earnest. Your thoughts are running after other things, when you pretend to pray to God. Away hypocrite! Go no further! It is in vain to strive any longer!" Here now, if you are not well informed in your understanding, you will presently cry out, "The Lord has forsaken me, the Lord has forgotten me" (Isaiah 49:14). Whereas, if you are rightly informed and enlightened, you will say, "Well, I will seek the Lord, and wait; I will not stop praying though the Lord keeps silent and speaks not a word of comfort. He loved Jacob dearly, and yet He made him wrestle before he had the blessing (see Genesis 32, Isaiah 40).

Seeming delays in God are not tokens of His displeasure. He may hide His face from His dearest saints. "I will wait for the Lord, who is hiding his face from the house of Jacob. I will put my trust in him" (Isaiah 8:17). He loves to help keep His people in prayer. He loves to find them ever knocking at the gate of heaven. "It may be," you can reason, "the Lord is trying me, or He loves to hear me groan out my condition before Him and solely rest upon Him for my needs."

PRAYER

Dear heavenly Father, I thank You that You desire honesty of expression in my prayer life. I thank You that I do not have to put on a hypocritical smiling front when I am in the deepest agony, but I can come to You just as I am in Jesus Christ. O Lord! I thank You because I am so aware of my personal shortcomings, inadequacies, and sins that sometimes I can only groan when I pray. Indeed, I have been unaware until now that You look upon my groanings, real honest moans from my soul, as real honest prayers. Thank You, God, for hearing my groans as prayers; now send Your Holy Spirit in Your redeeming love to remove the agony of my spirit and mind. I cannot form words to express my real spiritual needs, but You can see into my heart—so answer me! Through Jesus Christ, Your Son, Who knew the agonies of prayer. Amen.

—22—————————

PATIENCE IN PRAYER

The woman of Canaan would not take seeming denials for real ones. She knew that the Lord was gracious, and that the Lord would avenge His people though He bear long with them.

> Then Jesus told His disciples a parable to show them that they should always pray and not give up. He said: "In a certain town there was a judge who neither feared God nor cared about men. And there was a widow in that town who kept coming to him with the plea, 'Grant me justice against my adversary.'
> For some time he refused. But finally he said to himself, 'Even though I don't fear God or care about men, yet because this widow keeps bothering me, I will see that she gets justice, so that she won't eventually wear me out with her coming!' "

And the Lord said, "Listen to what the unjust judge says. And will not God bring about justice for his chosen ones, who cry out to him day and night? Will he keep putting them off?" (Luke 18:1-7)

The Lord has waited a lot longer upon me than I have waited upon Him! "I waited patiently for the Lord," David said; "he turned to me and heard my cry" (Psalm 40:1). The best remedy for patient waiting is to have your understanding well informed and enlightened.

Alas! How many poor souls are there in the world, who, because they are not well informed in their understanding, are often ready to give up all for lost upon almost every trick and temptation of Satan! The Lord pity them! The Lord help them to pray with the Spirit and with the understanding also.

This has been true to much of mine own experiences. When I have been in my fits of agony of spirit, I have often been strongly persuaded to quit, and to ask the Lord no longer to answer my request. But when I have remembered and understood what great sinners the Lord has had mercy upon, and how large His promises were still to sinners; and that it was not the whole and healthy, but the sick; not the righteous, but the sinners; not the full, but the empty that He intended to give His grace and mercy, then I renewed my patience and I persevered in prayer until I received the blessing. Remembering and understanding the teachings of the Scriptures made to me through the assistance of the Holy Spirit to cleave to Him, to hang upon Him, and continue to cry, though for the present He made no answer—and He helped me!

May the Lord help all of His poor, tempted and afflicted people to do the same and to continue, though it be long, according to the saying of the prophet: "For the revelation awaits an appointed time; it speaks of the end and will not prove false. Though it linger, wait for it; it will certainly come and will not delay" (Habakkuk 2:3). May the Lord help those to pray to that end, not by the inventions of men and their stinted forms, but with the Spirit and the understanding also.

PRAYER

O Lord, teach me patience and endurance in my prayers. Teach me not only those things I am to pray for, but teach me the promises of Scripture which I may claim as I pray. Guide me with Your Spirit in my heartfelt pleas for answers to my prayers. Grant me understanding when I pray day after day and You postpone Your answer. O Lord, I thank You for Your goodness and mercy. Help me to glorify and honour You before men and angels, even when my requests are not immediately fulfilled. Help me in all things and in all circumstances to live and pray as a Christian so others may see and understand You and Your Good News for all. Amen.

—23—————————————

WHEN YOU TRY BUT CANNOT PRAY

Now some of you may have experienced going in secret and intending to pray and pour out your soul before God, but found that you could scarcely pray anything at all.

Ah! Sweet soul! It is not your words that God so much regards. He will not mind if you cannot come to Him in some eloquent oration. His eye is on the brokenness of your heart; this is what makes the very heart of God to run over. Remember what God promised through David "The sacrifices of God are a broken spirit; a broken and contrite heart, O God, you will not despise" (Psalm 51:17).

The stopping of your words to God may arise from too much trouble in your heart. David was so troubled sometimes that he could not speak: "I remembered you, O God, and I groaned; I mused, and my spirit grew faint. You kept my eyes from closing; I was too troubled to speak" (Psalm 77:3,4). This might comfort all sorrowful hearts, that though you cannot through the anguish of your spirit speak much, yet the Holy Spirit stirs up in your heart groans and sighs so much more effectively. When your mouth is hindered, with the Holy Spirit your spirit is not hindered. Moses made heaven ring with his prayers, yet not one word came from his mouth in his deepest agony of heart.

If you would more fully express yourself before the Lord, study: first, your filthy estate; second, God's promises; and third, the loving heart of Christ. You may discern the heart of Christ by pondering His condescension and shed blood. You may think of the mercy He has shown to sinners in former times. Then in your prayer plead your own vileness and unworthiness, bemoan your condition before God, plead Christ's shed blood by expostulation, plead for the mercy that He extended to other sinners, plead with His many rich promises of grace, and let these things be upon your heart in your meditations.

Yet, let me still counsel you. Take heed that you do not content yourself with your mere words. Take heed lest you think that God looks only upon your words. Whether your words be few or many, let your heart and soul go with them to God. You shall seek and find Him when you seek Him with your whole heart and being:

> "For I know the plans I have for you," declares the Lord, "plans to prosper you and not to harm you, plans to give you hope and a future. Then you will call upon me and come and pray to me, and I will listen to you. You will seek me and find me when you seek me with all your heart. " (Jeremiah 29:11-13)

PRAYER

O Lord, I have not known how to come to You when I have been feeling the vileness and the condemnation of my sin. I have not felt able to ask You for a blessing when I have harboured unconfessed sin. By the Holy Spirit's help, enable me to examine my life and the depths of my heart so I can confess my sins and be forgiven. Create in me a clean heart so I can work and pray from pure motives and intentions. Lift me up so I might see how precious Christ is, experience His redeeming love in my heart, and be empowered to serve Him with greater boldness. Amen.

—24————————————

PRAY FOR THE HOLY SPIRIT

Christ bids us to pray for the Spirit, but this implies that a person without the Spirit may pray and be heard:

> So I say to you: Ask and it will be given to you; seek and you will find; knock and the door will be opened to you. For everyone who asks receives; he who seeks finds; and to him who knocks, the door will be opened. Which of you fathers, if your son asks for a fish, will give him a snake instead? Or if he asks for an egg, will give him a scorpion? If you then, though you are evil, know how to give good gifts to your children, how much more will your Father in heaven give the Holy Spirit to those who ask him!
> (Luke 11:9-13)

The speech of Christ in this passage is directed to

His own disciples. Christ is telling them that God would give His Holy Spirit to those who ask Him and He is to be understood as meaning to get *more* of the Holy Spirit. Since they are the disciples who are spoken to, they had a measure of the Spirit already. He had told His disciples to pray "Our Father". Christians ought to pray for the Holy Spirit; that is, they should pray for more of Him though God had endued them with Him already.

I might be asked, "Would you have no one pray except those who know that they are disciples of Christ?" I answer, "Yes." Let every soul that would be saved pour out his soul to God, though that soul cannot therefore conclude that he is a child of God.

I know that if the grace of God is in you, it will be natural for you to groan out your condition to God; as natural as it is for a sucking child to cry out for the breast of his mother. Prayer is one of the first things to reveal that a person is a Christian. But yet, if it be the right kind of prayer it will be as follows:

1. Right prayer must desire God in Christ, for Himself; for His holiness, love, wisdom and glory. Right prayer will run to God only through Christ, so that it will centre on Him and on Him alone. As the psalmist has prayed: "Whom have I in heaven but you? And earth has nothing I desire besides you" (Psalm 73:25).
2. Right prayer must enjoy continually communion with Him, both here and hereafter. "And I—in righteousness I shall see your face; when I awake, I shall be satisfied with seeing your likeness" (Psalm 17:15). And as Paul wrote, "Meanwhile we groan" (2 Corinthians 5:2).
3. Right prayer is accompanied with a continual labour after that which is prayed for. "My soul waits for the Lord more than watchmen wait for the morning, more than watchmen wait for the morning" (Psalm 130:6). For mark, I beseech you, there are two things that provoke to prayer. The one is a detestation to sin, and the things of this life; the other is a longing desire after

communion with God in a holy and undefiled state and inheritance. Compare but this one thing with most of the prayers that people make, and you shall find them but mock prayers, and the breathings of an abominable spirit; for even most either do not pray at all, or else they only endeavour to mock God and the world by doing so. Only compare their prayer and the course of their lives together, and you may easily see that the thing included in their prayer is the least looked after in their lives.

PRAYER

O Lord, I thank You for the gift of Your Holy Spirit in my life, but I confess that I have often pushed Him off into a corner of my life and I have grieved Him for my disregard of Him. Forgive me for my selfishness and my insensitivity to the spiritual blessings You would have me enjoy, because I have been too enraptured by the earthy and material. Fill me now with the fullness of Your Spirit, not for my selfish enjoyment, but for my communion with You—that will lead to Your praise and glory. Fill me with Your Spirit even now, that I might live a life consistent with my profession of faith in Jesus Christ. Amen.

— 25

PRAYER IN FEAR AND HOPE

Prayer is the duty of every one of the children of God. Since prayer is to be carried on by the Spirit of Christ in the soul, everyone who takes it upon himself to pray to the Lord needs to be wary and go about the work especially with the dread of God, as well as with the hope of the mercy of God through Christ.

Prayer is an ordinance of God in which you draw very near to God; therefore, your prayer must call for the assistance of the grace of God to help you pray, because in prayer you are especially in the presence of God.

It is a shame for a person to behave himself irreverently before a king, but it is a sin to behave so before God! And just as a wise king is not pleased with an oration made up with unseemly words and gestures, so God takes no pleasure in the sacrifice of fools:

Guard your steps when you go to the house of God. Go near to listen rather than to offer

the sacrifice of fools, who do not know that
they do wrong.
  Do not be quick with your mouth,
  do not be hasty in your heart
  to utter anything before God.
  God is in heaven
  and you are on earth,
  so let your words be few.
  As a dream comes when there are many
      cares,
    so the speech of a fool when there are
      many words.
When you make a vow to God, do not delay
in fulfilling it. He has no pleasure in fools;
fulfil your vow.
(Ecclesiastes 5:1-4)

Neither long discourses nor eloquent tongues are
pleasing to the ear of God, but a humble, broken and
contrite heart is sweet in the mind of the heavenly Majesty:

For this is what the high and lofty One says—
he who lives for ever, whose name is holy:
"I live in a high and holy place,
but also with him who is contrite and lowly in
    spirit,
to revive the spirit of the lowly
and to revive the heart of the contrite."
(Isaiah 57:15)

In some of the following pages I will discuss the chief
obstructions to right prayer.
    When men regard iniquity in their hearts, at the
time of their prayers before God, it is as though a great
impenetrable wall is separating them from God. "If I had
cherished sin in my heart," said the psalmist, "the Lord
would not have listened; but God has surely listened and
heard my voice in prayer" (Psalm 66:18,19).
    You must understand this: you may pray for the
prevention of temptation while at the same time you have a
secret love for the very thing which you are praying to resist

and are asking strength against. This is the wickedness of man's heart: it will even love and hold fast to that which with the mouth it prays against. This sort are those who honour God with their mouth, but their hearts are far from Him: "My people come to you, as they usually do, and sit before you to listen to your words, but they do not put them into practice. With their mouths they express devotion, but their hearts are greedy for unjust gain" (Ezekiel 33:31).

O! How ugly it would be in our eyes if we should see a beggar ask for alms with the intention of throwing it to the dogs! Or, what of that man who prays with one breath: "Bestow this upon me," and with the next, "I beseech You do not give it to me!" And yet, thus it is with those type of people who say with their mouths, "Thy will be done," and with their hearts they mean everything less. With their mouth they say, "Hallowed be Thy Name," and with their hearts and lives they delight to dishonour Him all the day long. These are the prayers that become sin, and though they put them up often, the Lord will never answer them. "They cried for help, but there was no one to save them—to the Lord, but he did not answer" (2 Samuel 22:42).

When people pray for a show, to be heard, and to be thought of as a somebody in religion, etc., these prayers also fall short of God's acceptance and are never likely to be answered in reference to eternal life. There are those who seek repute and applause for their eloquent words and who seek more to tickle the ears and heads of their hearers than anything else. These people pray to be heard by others, and have all of their reward already (see Matthew 6:5). You can discover these persons by:

1. Their eye is only on their auditory expressions.
2. They look for commendation when they are done.
3. Their hearts either rise or fall according to their praise or amount of enlargement.
4. The length of their prayers pleases them, and in order for their prayers to be long they will vainly repeat things over and over again (see Matthew 6:7).

5. When their prayers are over, they wait not to hear from God but from man.

PRAYER

Father, search me and know me. Reveal to me the hidden secrets of my heart. Show me the sin which I still love, and convict me by Your Spirit of all unrighteousness. Aid me to turn from all unrighteousness to You with the resolve to be obedient in all things. Forgive me and enable me to live moment by moment in love and faith. May these words of mine not be so much for the hearts and minds of others, but may they be from my heart to You and help others to give their hearts to You as well. Amen.

—26

PRAYER THAT ASSURES NO ANSWER

Prayer that God will not accept and answer is that prayer which is for the wrong things; or if for the right things, the prayer is with the wrong motives. Some come to God in prayer for that which they can spend upon their lusts or for the wrong ends. Some have not because they ask not, and others ask and have not because they ask amiss, that they may consume it on their lusts:

> You want something but don't get it. You kill and covet, but you cannot have what you want. You quarrel and fight. You do not have, because you do not ask God. When you ask, you do not receive, because you ask with wrong motives, that you may spend what you get on your pleasures. You adulterous people, don't you know that friendship with the world is hatred toward

God? Anyone who chooses to be a friend of
the world becomes an enemy of God.
(James 4:2-4)

Ends and purposes contrary to God's will are a
great argument with God for Him *not* to answer the
petitions you present to Him. Hence, so many pray for this
or that, and yet receive not. God answers them only with
silence. They have their words for their labour—and that is
all.

Now some might object and say that God does hear
some persons, though their hearts be not right with Him, as
He did Israel. He gave them quails in the wilderness though
they spent them upon their lusts. Yet, I answer that if God
does this it is in judgment and not in mercy. He gave them
their desire indeed, but they would have been better without
it, for He also sent leanness into their souls. Woe be to that
man when God answers Him in such a way! As the
psalmist explains:

Then they believed his promises
and sang his praise.
But they soon forgot what he had done
and did not wait for his counsel.
In the desert they gave in to their craving;
in the wasteland they put God to the test.
So he gave them what they asked for,
but sent a wasting disease upon them.
(Psalm 106:12-15)

There are other sorts of prayers that are not
answered. These are the prayers that are made by men and
presented to God in their own persons only, without their
appearing in the Lord Jesus. For though God has appointed
prayer, and promised to hear the prayers of His creatures,
yet He will not hear the prayer of any creature if he does not
come in Christ. Jesus has told us, "And I will do whatever
you ask in my name, so that the Son may bring glory to the
Father" (John 14:13). And as Paul has written, "And
whatever you do, whether in word or deed, do it all in the
name of the Lord Jesus, giving thanks to God the Father

through him" (Colossians 3:17). Though you never be so devout, earnest, zealous, and constant in prayer, yet it is in Christ only that you will be heard and accepted.

But alas! Most people do not know what it is to come to God in the Name of the Lord Jesus, and that is the reason why they live wicked, pray wicked, and die wicked.

PRAYER

O Lord, help me to pray with right motives and intentions in my heart. Help me never to ask for things so that I can simply spend those things upon my lusts or for the increase of my pleasures. Instead of praying wrongly, help me to know You so well that I will pray only for those things that You would want me to have and pray for. Help me to pray for those things that are according to Your will and intentions each day. Father, You see the larger scene. You see and understand my real needs and the needs of others. You know the real needs of Your Kingdom on earth. Help me to be Your co-worker in all of these things that You see so clearly. Fill me with Your Holy Spirit so that I can pray in Jesus' Name and make a real difference in the world. I offer this prayer not in my own righteousness, but in the righteousness of Your Son Who died for me. Amen.

— 27 —

PRAYER MUST HAVE POWER

The last thing which hinders prayer is the form of prayer without the power. It is an easy thing for people to be very hot for such things as forms of prayer, as they are written in a book. Yet they are altogether forgetful to inquire within themselves whether or not they have the spirit and power of prayer. These people are like a painted man, and their prayers are like a false voice. They appear as hypocrites in person, and their prayers are an abomination: "If any man turns a deaf ear to the law, even his prayers are detestable" (Proverbs 28:9). When they say they have been pouring out their souls to God, He says that they have been howling like dogs: "They do not cry out to me from their hearts but wail upon their beds. They gather together for grain and new wine but turn away from me" (Hosea 7:14).

When therefore you intend to pray to the Lord of heaven and earth, consider the following particulars:

1. Consider seriously what you want. Do not, as

many who in their words only beat the air, ask for such things as indeed you do not desire, nor see that you stand in need of.

2. When you see what you want, keep to that and take heed to pray sensibly.

3. Take heed that your heart goes out to God as well as your mouth. Let not your mouth go any further than you strive to draw out your heart along with it. David would lift his heart and soul to the Lord; and for good reason, for so far as a man's mouth goes along without his heart, so far his prayer is but lip-labour only. If you have in mind to enlarge in prayer before God, see to it that it be with your heart.

4. Avoid just affecting expressions and pleasing yourself with their use, because you can quickly forget the real life of prayer.

PRAYER

Father, my prayer to You will never have power without the Holy Spirit filling my life and until I really begin to praise You for Who you are and for what You are doing according to Your holy character. I love You for creating the wonder of life and the beauty of creation. I thank You for the Word that proclaims many things which are hidden from those who think they are wise in their own eyes, but which make wise those who are humble and contrite of heart. Grant me power in prayer by giving me a greater sensibility of Your Wonder, Majesty, and Love in Christ Jesus. Amen.

—28

A WORD OF ENCOURAGEMENT

Take heed that you do not throw off prayer through sudden persuasions that you have not the Holy Spirit. It is the great work of the devil to do his best, or rather worst, against the best prayers. He will flatter false concealing hypocrites and feed them with a thousand fancies of well-doing, when their very duties of prayer, and all their other duties as well, stink in the nostrils of God. The devil will also stand at a poor Joshua's hand to resist him; that is, to persuade him that neither his person nor his performance are accepted by God.

> Then he showed me Joshua the high priest standing before the angel of the Lord, and Satan standing at his right side to accuse him. The Lord said to Satan, "The Lord rebuke you, Satan! The Lord, who has chosen Jerusalem, rebuke you! Is not this man a burning stick snatched from the fire?"

Now Joshua was dressed in filthy clothes as he stood before the angel. The angel said to those who were standing before him, "Take off his filthy clothes." Then he said to Joshua, "See, I have taken away your sin, and I will put rich garments on you." Then I said, "Put a clean turban on his head." So they put a clean turban on his head and clothed him, while the angel of the Lord stood by. The angel of the Lord gave this charge to Joshua: "This is what the Lord Almighty says: 'If you will walk in my ways and keep my requirements, then you will govern my house and have charge of my courts, and I will give you a place among those standing here' " (Zechariah 3:1-7).

Take heed, therefore, of such false conclusions and groundless discouragements; and though such persuasions do come in upon your spirit to convince you that you cannot pray, rather than being discouraged by them use them to put yourself into greater sincerity and restlessness of spirit when you approach God.

As such sudden temptations should not stop you from prayer and pouring out your soul to God; so neither should your own heart's corruptions hinder you. It may be that you find within all those corruptions before mentioned, and they may be endeavouring to put themselves in you when you seek to pray to Him. Your business then is to judge them and to pray against them. Lay yourself much more at the foot of God in a sense of your own vileness rather than arguing for your requests from the vileness and corruption of your heart. Plead with God for justifying and sanctifying grace, and don't argue from discouragement and despair. David prayed this way: "For the sake of your name, O Lord, forgive my iniquity, though it be great" (Psalm 25:11).

I would like to speak a word of encouragement to the poor, tempted and cast–down soul to pray to God in Christ. Though all prayer that is accepted by God in reference to eternal life must be in the Spirit—for that only makes intercession for us according to the will of God—yet because many poor souls may have the Holy Spirit working on them, and stirring them up to groan unto the Lord for mercy, they may pray to God through Christ. Even though through unbelief they do not, nor for the present cannot, believe that they are the people of God, such people as He delights in, still the truth of grace may be coming upon them.

That Scripture in Luke 11 is very encouraging to any poor soul who hungers after Jesus Christ. In verses 5-7, Jesus speaks a parable about a man who went to his friend to borrow three loaves, who, because he was in bed denied him; yet for his importunity, he did rise and give him what he asked. This parable clearly signifies that though poor souls, through the weakness of their faith, cannot see that they are the friends of God, yet they should never quit asking, seeking and knocking at God's door for mercy. Poor heart! You cry out that God will not regard you, and then you find that you are not a friend of His but rather an enemy in your heart through wicked words and works. And you are as though you heard the Lord saying to you: "Trouble me not! I cannot give to you as to the one in the parable." Yet, I say continue knocking, crying, bemoaning and wailing. My own experience tells me that nothing will so prevail with God as beseeching. Is it not so with you respecting beggars who come to your door? Though you have no heart to give them anything at their first asking, yet if they follow you bemoaning themselves, won't you give to them? Scripture tells us that God will arise and give us what we need.

PRAYER

O Lord, may I forgive others that You might forgive me. O Lord, may I give to the needy that You might meet my daily needs. I come today by faith and ask that You fill me with Your Holy Spirit as a gift of Your grace. Grant unto me the spirit of perseverance that I might prevail in my prayers and requests before You whenever those requests are according to Your will. And empower me as well to give unto others the encouragement which You have given to me in Jesus. Amen.

— 29

PRAYER BEFORE THE THRONE OF GRACE

Another encouragement for a poor trembling convicted soul is to consider the place, throne, or seat on which the great God has placed Himself to hear the petitions and prayers of poor creatures—and that is the throne of grace or the mercy seat. "Let us then approach the throne of grace with confidence, so that we may receive mercy and find grace to help us in our time of need" (Hebrews 4:16).

In these days of the Gospel, God has taken up His seat, His abiding-place, in mercy and forgiveness; and from His throne of grace He intends to hear the sinner and to commune with him. Poor souls! They are very apt to entertain strange thoughts of God and His bearing towards them, and suddenly conclude that God will have no regard unto them when yet He is upon His mercy seat. God has taken up His place there on purpose, to the end that He may hear and regard the prayers of poor creatures. If He had said, "I will commune with you from My throne of judgment," then indeed you might have trembled and fled from the great and glorious Majesty. But when He says that He will hear and commune with souls upon the throne of grace, or upon the mercy seat, this should encourage you and cause you to hope. Come boldly to the throne of grace!

As there is a mercy seat from whence God is willing to commune with poor sinners, so there is also by His seat Jesus Christ. Jesus Christ is continually sprinkling the mercy seat with His blood. As Scripture says: "You have come to God, the judge of all men, to the spirits of righteous men made perfect, to Jesus the mediator of a new covenant, and to the sprinkled blood that speaks a better word than the blood of Abel" (Hebrews 12:23-24).

When the high priest under the law was to go into the holiest, where the mercy seat was, he could not go in without blood (see Hebrews 9:7). Why so? Because God was on the mercy seat, yet He was perfectly just as well as merciful. Now the blood was to stop justice from running out upon the persons concerned in the intercession of the high priest (see Leviticus 16:13-17). This should signify to you that all your unworthiness should not hinder you from coming to God in Christ for mercy. You cry out that you are vile, and therefore God will not regard your prayers. It is true, if you delight in your vileness and come to God in mere pretence. But if from a sense of your vileness you do pour out your heart to God, desiring to be saved from your guilt, and cleansed from all your filth, with all your heart; fear not, for your vileness will not cause the Lord to stop His ear from hearing you. The value of the blood of Christ which is sprinkled upon the mercy seat stops the course of justice, and opens a floodgate for the mercy of the Lord to be extended unto you.

Jesus is there before God, not only to sprinkle the mercy seat with His blood, but He speaks, and His blood speaks. Jesus has an audience, and His blood has an audience; insomuch that God says when He sees the blood, He will pass over you (see Exodus 12). Be sober and humble. Go to the Father in the Name of His Son and tell Him your case. Go in the assistance of the Spirit and with your understanding also in accordance with the Word of God.

PRAYER

Dear heavenly Father, Father of light and truth, I thank You that during this time when the Gospel is being preached around the world, You are seated upon a mercy seat, the throne of grace. I thank You that I can come to You through the shed blood of Jesus Christ, and that I do not have to feel the threat of deserved judgment because of His intercession for me. Help me now to share this precious Good News that many might be saved through faith. Amen.

—30—

DO NOT GRIEVE THE HOLY SPIRIT

There is and must be a sad reproof for those who never pray at all. "I will pray," said the Apostle, and so say all Christians. You are not a Christian if you are not a praying person. The promise of God is that everyone who is righteous will pray: "Therefore let everyone who is godly pray to you while you may be found; surely when the mighty waters rise, they will not reach him" (Psalm 32:6). You then are a wicked wretch if you do not pray!

Jacob got the name of Israel by wrestling with God in prayer: "Then the man said, 'Your name will no longer be Jacob, but Israel, because you have struggled with God and with men and have overcome'" (Genesis 32:28). And all of his children have borne that name with him: "Peace and mercy to all who follow this rule, even to the Israel of God" (Galatians 6:16).

But the people who forget prayer, who call not upon the Name of the Lord, they have prayers made for them, but they are prayers such as this: "Pour out your wrath on the nations that do not acknowledge you, on the peoples who do not call on your name" (Jeremiah 10:25). Are you like these people who do not call upon the Name of the Lord? Do you go to bed like a dog and rise like a hog, or a sot, and forget to call upon God? What will you do when you are damned in hell, because you could not find it in your heart to pray to God and ask for heaven? Who will be there to grieve for your sorrow, because you didn't count the mercy of God worth asking for? I tell you that the ravens and the dogs shall rise up in judgment against you, for they will, according to their kind, make signs and a noise for something to refresh them when they want it. But you have not the heart to ask for heaven or approach our great God in prayer when He is upon His throne of grace. Though you must eternally perish in hell, if you do not ask God for heaven, you ask Him not.

What about you who make it your business to slight, mock at, and undervalue the Spirit and praying by the Holy Spirit? What will you do when God calls you to account for these things? You count it high treason to speak a word against the king, nay, you tremble at the thought of it; and yet in the meantime you blaspheme the Spirit of the Lord. Is God indeed to be dallied with, and will the end be pleasant with you? Did God send the Holy Spirit into the hearts of His people so that they could taunt Him; especially when He calls them to prayer? Is this to serve God? Does this demonstrate the reformation of your church? Can you be content to be damned for your sins against the Law, and can you add to this your sin against the Holy Spirit?

Must the holy, harmless and undefiled Spirit of grace, the nature of God, the promise of Christ, the Comforter of His children, the One without Whom no one can be acceptable to the Father—must this, I say, be the burden of your song, to taunt, deride, and mock at Him? If God sent Korah and his company headlong into hell for speaking against Moses and Aaron, do you who mock the Spirit of Christ think you can escape unpunished (see Numbers 16 and Hebrews 10)? Did you never read what God did to Ananias and Sapphira for telling but one lie to the Holy Spirit (see Acts 5)? Also to Simon Magus for undervaluing Him and His work (see Acts 8)? And will your sin be a virtue, or go unrewarded with vengeance, if you make it your business to rage against, and oppose His office, service and help that He gives to the children of God in prayer? It is a fearful thing to oppose and despise the Spirit of grace, Who would bless your life and your prayers.

As this is the doom of those who do openly blaspheme the Holy Spirit, in a day of disdain and reproach to His office and service, so also it is sad for you who resist the spirit of prayer by using forms of men's inventing. A very juggle of the devil, that the traditions of men should be better esteemed than the spirit of prayer. Is this any less than the accursed abomination of Jereboam, who kept many from going to Jerusalem, the place and way of God's appointment to worship? One would think that God's judgments of old upon the hypocrites of that day would make those who have heard of it to take heed and fear to do the same. Yet the doctors of our day are so far from taking the warning of this punishment of others that they most desperately rush into the same transgression by placing their traditions above the Scriptures and their written prayers above praying in the spirit. They set up institutions of men, neither commanded nor commended by God, and then they say that whosoever will not obey them must be run from the land or from this world. Thus is the spirit of prayer disowned, and the form of the printed prayer imposed, the Spirit debased, and the form extolled.

Those who pray with the Spirit, though ever so humble and holy, are counted as fanatics. Those who pray with the form of a written prayer only, and without the Spirit, are counted virtuous. And how will those in favour of such a practice answer that Scripture which commands that the Church turn away from such people who have a form of godliness and deny the power of it (see 2 Timothy 3:5)?

PRAYER

O Lord, I live in a different time from that of John Bunyan, who was forced by law and by ecclesiastical authorities to pray and worship You in a certain manner and formality, and who was imprisoned for his disobedience. And yet, I find that the temptation is always before me to honour men and the works of men far more than You. Forgive me for those times when I have rejected the influence of the Holy Spirit, Who was calling me from sin and to prayer. Today, I resolve to be sensitive to His leading, so I can pray to You at His bidding. Amen.

— 31—

PUT GOD BEFORE MAN

He who advances the *Book of Common Prayer* above the spirit of prayer advances a form of men's prayer above the Holy Spirit's leading and influence. This do all who banish, or desire to banish, those who pray with the spirit of prayer while they hug and embrace those who pray with the form only, and that because they use the *Book of Common Prayer*. Therefore they love and advance the form of their own or others' inventing, before the spirit of prayer, which is God's special and gracious appointment.

Look into the jails of England and into the ale-houses, and I know that you will find those who plead for the spirit of prayer in the jails, and those who look after the form of men's inventions only in the ale-houses. It is evident also by the silencing of God's dear ministers, though never so powerfully enabled by the spirit of prayer, if they in conscience cannot admit of that form of Common Prayer. If this be not an exalting of the *Common Prayer Book* above either praying by the Spirit or preaching the Word, I have taken my mark amiss. It is not pleasant for me to dwell on this. The Lord in mercy turn the hearts of the people to seek more after the spirit of prayer and in the strength of that, to pour out their souls before the Lord. Only let me say it is a sad sign that that which is one of the most eminent parts of the pretended worship of God is anti-Christian when it has nothing but the tradition of men and the strength of persecution to uphold or plead for it.

I shall conclude with a word of advice to all God's people.

1. Believe that as sure as you are in the way of God that you will meet with temptations.
2. The first day therefore that you enter into Christ's congregation look for temptations to come.
3. When temptations do come, beg of God to carry you through them.
4. Be jealous of your own heart, and do not let it deceive you in your evidences of heaven or in your walking with God in this world.
5. Take heed of the flatteries of false brethren.
6. Keep in the life and power of the truth.
7. Look most at the things which are not seen.
8. Take heed of little sins.
9. Keep the promise of God warm upon your heart.
10. Renew your acts of faith in the blood of Christ.
11. Consider the work God has for your generation.
12. Resolve to run with the foremost of the godly of your generation.

Grace be with you.

THE SPIRIT OF PRAYER

Wouldst thou have that good, that blessed mind,
That is so much to heavenly things inclin'd

That it aloft will soar, and always be
Contemplating on the blest eternity.
That mind that never thinks itself at rest,
But when it knows it is for ever blest;
That mind that can be here no more content,
Than he that in the prison doth lament;
That blessed mind that counts itself then free
When it can at the throne with Jesus be,
There to behold the mansions He prepares
For such as be with Him and His co-heirs.
This mind is in the covenant of grace,
And shall be theirs that truly seek His face. [1]

PRAYER

O Lord, my God and Saviour, may I be strengthened
by Your Spirit and by all that I have learned from John
Bunyan, who suffered intense and lengthy persecution for
his faith. May I be strengthened in my mind by the words of
teaching and admonition he has proclaimed from the
Scriptures, that I might love You with all of my mind. May I
be strengthened in soul and spirit by Your Spirit of truth
working in my life, that I might love you with all my soul
and strength. May I be strengthened in my heart whenever I
am tempted to place the traditions of men above Your Word
and Spirit. Strengthen me and fill me with Your Spirit so I
can better and more courageously witness to others about
Your redeeming love and the life-transforming power of
Your gospel. For the sake of Your kingdom, Amen.

---

1. From *Ebal and Gerizim,* a lengthy poem by John Bunyan that
included the short poem, *The Spirit of Prayer.*

JOHN BUNYAN'S DYING WORDS
ON PRAYER

Before you enter into prayer, ask your soul these questions:

1. To what end, O my soul, am I retired into this place? Am I come to discourse with the Lord in prayer? Is He present, will He hear me? Is He merciful, will He help me? Is my business with Him unimportant, is it concerning the welfare of my soul? What words will I use to move Him to compassion?
2. To make your preparation complete consider that you are but dust and ashes, and He is the great God and Father of our Lord Jesus Christ. He clothes himself with light as with a garment, and you are but a vile sinner. He is a Holy God, and you are but a crawling worm. He is the omnipotent Creator.
3. In all your prayers do not forget to thank God for all of His mercies.
4. When you pray, rather let your heart be without words than your words be without heart.
5. Prayer will make a man cease from sin or sin will entice a man to cease from prayer.
6. The spirit of prayer is more precious than treasures of gold and silver.
7. Pray often, for prayer is a shield to the soul, a sacrifice to God, and a scourge to Satan.

THE LORD'S PRAYER IN VERSE

Our Father which in heaven art,
  Thy Name be always hallowed;
Thy kingdom come, Thy will be done;
  Thy heavenly path be followed
  By us on earth as 'tis with Thee,
We humbly pray;
  And let our bread us given be,
From day to day.
Forgive our debts as we forgive
  Those that to us indebted are:
Into temptation lead us not,
  But save us from the wicked snare.
The kingdom's Thine, the power too.
  We Thee adore;
The glory also shall be Thine
  For evermore.

By John Bunyan
Date unknown

MANSOUL'S PETITION TO EMMANUEL

O our Lord and Sovereign Prince Emmanuel, the potent, the long-suffering Prince: grace is poured into Thy lips, and to Thee belongs mercy and forgiveness, though we have rebelled against Thee. We who are no more worthy to be called Thy Mansoul, nor yet fit to partake of common benefits, do beseech Thee, and Thy Father by Thee to do away our transgressions. We confess that Thou mightest cast us away for them, but do it not for Thy Name's sake; let the Lord rather take an opportunity at our miserable condition, to let out His bowels and compassions to us; we are compassed on every side, Lord, our own backslidings reprove us; our Diabolonians within our town fright us, and the army of the angel of the bottomless pit distresses us. Thy grace can be our salvation, and whither to go but to Thee we know not.

Furthermore, O gracious Prince, we have weakened our captains, and they are discouraged, sick, and of late some of them grievously worsted and beaten out of the field by the power and force of the tyrant. Yea, even those of our captains in whose valour we did formerly use to put most of our confidence, they are as wounded men. Besides Lord, our enemies are lively, and they are strong, they vaunt and boast themselves, and do threaten to part us among themselves for a booty. They are fallen also upon us, Lord, with many thousand Doubters, such as with whom we cannot tell what to do; they are all grim-looked, and unmerciful ones, and they bid defiance to us and Thee.

Our wisdom is gone, our power is gone, because Thou art departed from us, nor have we what we may call ours but sin, shame, and confusion of face for sin. Take pity upon us, O Lord, take pity upon us, Thy miserable town of Mansoul, and save us out of the hands of our enemies. Amen.

From John Bunyan's THE HOLY WAR
First published in 1682

A NOTE ON THE TEXT

The material on prayer in this book is taken from *The Whole Works of John Bunyan*, edited by George Offor and published in London by Blackie and Sons in 1875. In editing the thirty-one meditations, I have completely modernised the text, shortened sentences, and changed obsolete words, such as the word "vizard". The meditation titles are my own, as well as the divisions into the thirty-one meditations. The meditations are taken from Bunyan's discourse *On Praying in the Spirit*. In many cases, I have quoted Bunyan's Scripture references entirely where it has proved helpful. I believe the text is true to what Bunyan would want it to be for the twentieth-century reader, and I hope that the devotional format will attract more readers of Bunyan's fine material on prayer than otherwise would have been the case.

I have capitalised all references to Deity when referred to by a pronoun in Bunyan's text. *How to Pray in the Spirit* is a completely revised edition of my *Pilgrim's Prayer Book* by John Bunyan, which was published by Tyndale House Publishers: Wheaton, Illinois, in January, 1986. It went out of print in 1987, when Tyndale House discontinued its Living Classics Series. In 1990, it was reprinted in a Japanese translation.

SCRIPTURE INDEX

GRACE ABOUNDING

John Bunyan

A lesser-known but still very relevant book by the author of *The Pilgrim's Progress, Grace Abounding* describes the grace of God towards Bunyan above his sins and Satan's temptations, recounting the support he received in his need. Again he is occupied with universal and eternal truths, commending not one individual opinion but in fact the object of all Christian teaching, Him who is the same yesterday, today and for ever.

The *Grace Abounding* which Bunyan extolled in the seventeenth century is the same grace in which we can all trust today.

Catalogue Number YB 9239   £3.50

THE PILGRIM'S PROGRESS

John Bunyan

As John Bunyan's most famous work, *The Pilgrim's Progress* has been a firm favourite over the centuries since it was written, and there is no class, educated or uneducated, to which this book would not appeal. The reason is that Bunyan unveils human nature and discloses the conflict of his own soul, writing out of the fullness of his heart, in a direct and simple way which has never been surpassed.

Bunyan's work refutes the theory that people need only believe and turn to God for their way to be made plain. The conflicts, sorrows and temptations which lie in wait for Christian in his travels are just as real for us at the end of the twentieth century. The pilgrimage taken by Christian and Faithful and Hopeful, Christiana and Mercy, is one which must still be taken by us all.

Catalogue Number YB 9238   £3.99